Marketing Dynamics

Marketing Educator's Handbook

Judy Commers, M.A.E.
Marketing Education Teacher-Coordinator
Porter County Career Center
Valparaiso, Indiana

Marketing Dynamics Text
Brenda Clark, Ed.D.
Jennie Sobel, M.B.A.
Cynthia Gendall Basteri, Ed.D.

Publisher
The Goodheart-Willcox Company, Inc.
Tinley Park, Illinois
www.g-w.com

Contents

Foundations for Classroom Success

Teaching is a rewarding but challenging profession. It often takes years of experience to figure out how best to handle the many challenging situations that arise during the school day. To save you time and frustration, we have compiled suggestions from experienced teachers on ways to make the teaching and learning experience as enjoyable and productive as possible.

This component of the *Marketing Dynamics* program is *The Marketing Educator's Handbook.* It consists of the *Foundations for Classroom Success,* the *Activity Buffet,* and *Resources for Marketing Educators.*

The *Foundations for Classroom Success* provides ideas and strategies to help you achieve goals for yourself as a teacher and for your students as learners. Topics include creating your mission statement, planning before the school year starts, strategies for effective teaching, building academic skills, connecting to the world of work, preparing students for work in the twenty-first century, and keeping yourself energized.

The *Activity Buffet* is a unique resource of generic activities that can be used with any chapter or any topic. The *Resources for Marketing Educators* lists a wide array of sources for teaching strategies, marketing content, professional organizations, and job search.

What Is Your Mission?

Before the school year starts, ask yourself these questions: Why am I a teacher? What is my mission? Your answers may include some or all of the following: you want to touch students' lives, make a difference in their futures, or other answers that focus on helping students. Many businesses, large and small, develop mission statements to help them focus on and achieve their goals. To help you stay focused, compose your own mission or vision statement. It can be as long or short, detailed or general, as you wish. Here is an example:

My mission is to offer a quality educational experience for each and every student and to help all students realize their potential.

When you are pleased with your mission statement, make a copy of it and post it where you can easily see it. If you are so inclined, you can embellish it graphically and have it framed. Read over your mission statement periodically for inspiration.

Before the School Year Starts

One of the keys to a successful school year is to plan *before* the school year starts. Plan your curriculum. Prepare yourself and your classroom. If you do most of your planning before the school year starts, you are likely to be better prepared and have more time during the school year. Once the students arrive at school, the schedule becomes very hectic; and it may be hard to find the time to plan and gather materials.

Plan Your Curriculum

Plan your entire course before the course starts. The procedure described below will help you do this. The benefit of this type of planning is that you know ahead of time how much time you have for the whole course, and you can decide how much time to spend on each topic. You are then able to make sure that the students have the opportunity to learn all the topics that you want them to learn during the course. You are also able to make sure that you have the materials for each class meeting and time to arrange for special events, such as job fairs, speakers, and field trips.

Curriculum Planning Process

The following steps will help you plan the curriculum for your course.

1. Identify the number of class meetings per week, minutes per class meeting, and first and last date of the course.

2. Gather curriculum materials, such as the textbook and objectives or performance indicators that must be covered.
3. Obtain monthly calendars for all the months during which you will teach this course. On these calendars, note all the in-service days, holidays, and any other days when students will not be in your class. If you and your students intend to compete in career and technical student organizations, also note those key dates.
4. Calculate how many teachable days you actually have. Analyze the time frame. Will the class meet for 50-minute periods five days a week, or 85-minute blocks three days a week? If you do not meet every day, cross off the days you do not meet on your calendars. Determine how much time you will have to actually teach.
5. Determine the content you want to cover. Use local objectives or the National Standards performance indicators.
6. Determine how much time you want to spend on each objective or performance indicator. Note on the calendar the topic and/or performance indicator to be covered on each class day.
7. Plan your assessments. See the section, "Assessment," pages 32, 35–37. Decide the types of assessments, including assignments and projects. You might find it valuable to have a test or quiz on the same day every week. Note on the calendar the test/quiz dates and assignment due dates.
8. Plan any special activities, such as speakers or field trips, and note the dates on your calendar.
9. If you will have a DECA chapter, note key DECA dates on your calendar.
10. If you will have a school-based enterprise, note key dates on your calendar, such as the grand opening.

You now have a plan for your entire course. Not only will these calendars help you be better prepared, they will also help your students plan their studying and assignments.

When you find out your students' birthdays, add them to your calendar. Embellish the calendars with clip art and quotations. See sample calendar, Figure H-1. For quotation suggestions, see *Activity Buffet—Warm-Ups*. Review the monthly calendars as you progress through the course, and adjust or add as necessary. At the beginning of each month, print enough calendars for all your students and distribute.

Using *Marketing Dynamics* **to Plan Curriculum**

The *Marketing Dynamics* package provides support to help you in this planning process. The "Introduction for Teachers" in the *Teacher's Edition* has a section "Planning Your Course." This section has four tables for four different course schedules. Each table suggests how to cover the chapters in the time allotted. For example, the course schedule for a trimester course of 12 weeks suggests that the first three chapters be covered in the first week.

In addition, the *Marketing Dynamics* student text is correlated with the *National Standards* for *Business Administration Core* and *Marketing Core*. These correlations appear in the "Introduction for Teachers" of the *Teacher's Edition* in the section "National Standards for Marketing Education." In this section, the national standards, performance elements, and performance indicators are listed by topic and correlated to the *Marketing Dynamics* student text. Also in the *Teacher's Edition* and in the *Teacher's Resources*, the performance indicators for each chapter are listed.

Contact Students and Parents

It is a great idea to contact both students and parents before school starts. Send each a letter conveying your excitement about the marketing course. This is an opportunity to impress both the parents and the students and to get them excited about the course, too.

In the letter to the parents, provide an overview of the course and describe its long-term benefits. It is also a good idea to include information about course requirements, grading system, and any fees. Some schools also require the student and parent to sign an Internet usage form. If you do not have access to the parents' addresses, distribute this information at the school's open house for parents. See sample parent letter, Figure H-2.

In the letter to the students, convey your excitement about their being in the marketing program. Tell them the times and days that the class meets. Preview some of the activities that students will find fun and exciting. If students are required to participate in a career and technical student organization, describe the organization and the types

(Continued on page 9)

September

HOLIDAYS **4** Labor Day **22-23** Rosh Hashanah (Jewish New Year)	**NEW SEASON** **23** Autumnal Equinox	**BIRTHDAY** **25** Ranell		**1** <u>**Student Day**</u> Test Orientation	**2**
3	**4** Labor Day No school Enjoy!	**5** What is marketing? MK:001 Ch1: 16-20	**6** Marketing functions MK:002 Ch1: 20-28	**7** Economic goods and services EC:002 Ch2: 31-35	**8** <u>**Student Day**</u> Quiz MK:001, 002 EC:002	**9**
10	**11** Business ownership and activities BL:003; EC:071 Ch2: 36-39	**12** Economic utilities EC:004; MK:002 Ch3: 42-48	**13** What is a market? IM:194, 196 Ch4: 51-56	**14** Role of business in society EC:070 Ch5: 65-68	**15** <u>**Student Day**</u> Test MK:001, 002; BL:003; EC:002, 004, 070, 071; IM:194, 196	**16**
17	**18** DECA Guidelines Elect officers	**19** DECA Plan Program of Work **Due:** Written Work 1	**20** Parliamentary Procedure	**21** Parliamentary Procedure CO:063, 141	**22** <u>**Student Day**</u> Quiz Parliamentary Procedure; CO:063, 141	**23**
24	**25** Ethics and fairness EI: 004, 021, 022, 029, 036	**26** Challenge Ed CO:119; EI:045 **Due:** Current Event Report 1	**27** DECA Civic Consciousness Project EI:030, 033	**28** <u>**Student Day**</u> Test Parliam.Proc; CO:063, 119, 141; EI:004, 021, 022, 029, 030, 033, 036, 045	**29** In-Service No school Enjoy!	**30**

"In the middle of difficulty lies opportunity."
Albert Einstein

Figure H-1. Class Calendar. Notice that this sample calendar includes topics for each day, performance indicator codes (e.g., MK:001), test and quiz days, DECA days, and assignment due dates.

Marketing Education

Judy Commers

•

Macon County
Career Center

•

1005 N. Main St.

•

Anytown, IN

•

46383

•

(555)
555-0170

•

FAX
(555)
555-0173

The Macon County Career Center marketing program is proud to sponsor the school's DECA youth group.

August 14, 20xx

Dear Parent or Guardian:

I am very pleased that your student has elected to enroll in the Marketing Foundations course at the Macon County Career Center. Marketing Foundations is a year-long course designed to prepare students for college or a career in marketing, entrepreneurship, or management.

In addition to class instruction in Marketing Foundations, your student will have the opportunity to join DECA—An Association of Marketing Students. DECA is an international student organization that sponsors competitions and community service. Membership in this organization provides the opportunity for students to experience leadership and learn skills in their career areas. The first round competitions will be held in January at the Gary Career Center, the state competitions in Indianapolis in February, and the National Conference in Anaheim, California, in April. As part of the learning experience, students will organize and run fund-raisers to help cover the costs of participating in the competitions.

Students who maintain a B average in this course will receive 6 hours of dual credit (high school and college) through Ivy Tech State College. We expect this college credit to be transferable to many other colleges and universities.

The fees for this course include the $15 membership fee for DECA (local and national) and a $30 course fee, which covers textbook rental and supplies. If you pay by check, please make two separate checks, each payable to Macon County Career and Technical Center. Your student can bring the payments to school, or you can send them to the Career Center.

Enclosed please find an overview of the Marketing Education Program at Macon County Career Center. It includes a program description, the course outline, and a detailed description of the grading system. The grading system is based on a mastery approach to learning. Please read this material carefully, as we want to be sure both you and your student understand how the mastery approach works. On the last page are spaces for the signatures of both you and your student. Also enclosed is a "Network and Internet Access Agreement for Students." Please also read this carefully and have you and your student sign the last page. Please have your student return both signed forms to me.

A letter will be sent to your student with the time schedule and other information.

If you have any questions or concerns, please contact me at the Career Center, 555-555-0170, or my home, 555-555-0197.

Sincerely,

Judy Commers

Mrs. Judy Commers
Marketing Foundations Teacher

Figure H-2. Parent Letter. Notice the positive tone of the letter and the key information provided, including how to contact the teacher.

of activities in which students might participate. See sample student letter, Figure H-3.

Although it is extra work to prepare this kind of letter for parents and students, it will pay off during the year. First, the parents will be impressed with your efforts. They will see how well prepared you are for the class. Second, you have an opportunity to show the parents that the course is a serious one that will require work and effort on their child's part. Third, you can explain the benefits that their child will get from working hard in the class and taking it seriously. The result is likely to be that the parents will have a positive feeling about the class and encourage their child to do his or her best in your classroom.

The letter to the students will also have a positive impact. It will show students that you care about them. The material you send them can show them that you are serious about the course and expect them to take the course seriously. The enthusiasm you show in the letter may get them excited about the course and eager to participate.

Prepare Yourself

A large part of the impact of a class depends on the impact of the teacher. Teachers need to remember that they are professionals and role models for their students. You are a professional, just like a medical doctor or a lawyer. Prominently display your teaching certificate. Your certificate shows that you worked hard to achieve a high level of expertise in teaching.

You know the saying, "There is only one time to make a good first impression." What impression will students receive when they look at you? How will you dress for class? Do you try to look like a teenager? Do you wear jeans because they are comfortable? You might want to consider wearing professional clothes that an executive would wear. Students will see you in this professional dress and get a glimpse of the professional business world. They will see that you take marketing and teaching them seriously.

Prepare Your Classroom

Your classroom will also make a lasting impression on your students. Even if you do not have your own classroom, try to have a space for marketing in the classroom, such as at least one bulletin board. Some of the suggestions for displays are portable, and you can make poster boards that you can set up during your class and store in a closet at other times.

Before the school year starts, decide how you want the desks arranged and how you want to assign seats. For each of your classes, create a seating chart. Figure H-4 shows a typical seating chart. You can reproduce this one or make one of your own. For the first day of school, make enough copies of the seating chart for each student in each class. Also make an overhead transparency.

One way to assign seats is to have each student draw a seat assignment from an envelope as he or she walks into the class. Figure H-5 can be reproduced and used to make the seat assignment slips. You might want to laminate the finished slips for durability.

For the first day, have a large "Welcome to Marketing" sign/banner or write it large on the board. Include on the sign or other prominent place the class name, your name, and any other welcoming and supporting information.

Since everyone likes to see his or her own name, make a name card for each student. Here are some name card ideas. If you have the students' names in a software program, print the names on labels in a fancy or unusual (but readable) typeface. Buy or make cards in a shape, such as a star, diamond, or sailboat. Place a student's name on each shape. Laminate each shape, and hang them with fishing line from the ceiling or place them on a wall or bulletin board. At a time of your choosing, have students take down their name cards and keep them if they wish.

Here are some suggestions for displays and bulletin boards: marketing logos; advertisements; interesting posters related to marketing and advertising; newspaper articles on a "Marketing in the News" bulletin board; articles on a "Status of the Economy" bulletin board; articles and images or ads for new products; inspiring quotations; posters encouraging good work and study habits; photos and biographies of important people in business, marketing, economics, and politics. You could organize the class into teams, and assign each team the responsibility for classroom displays and bulletin boards for a month.

Get Organized

Set up your classroom for ease of teaching. After you have developed your curriculum (see "Plan Your Curriculum," preceding) and your classroom management plan (see "Develop a Classroom Management Plan," following), go through both to determine what materials and

(Continued on page 13)

Marketing Education

Judy Commers

•

Macon County
Career Center

•

1005 N. Main St.

•

Anytown, IN

•

46383

•

(555)
555-0170

•

FAX
(555)
555-0173

The Macon County Career Center marketing program is proud to sponsor the school's DECA youth group.

August 14, 20xx

Dear Marketing Foundations Student:

Welcome to the Macon County Career Center! I hope this will be one of the most exciting experiences of your life. The Marketing Foundations course will provide many opportunities for you to participate in marketing as well as learn about it. I am very excited about having you in my Marketing Foundations class.

One of the requirements of this course is that you join DECA—An Association of Marketing Students. DECA is an international student organization that sponsors competitions and community service. Membership in this organization will provide you with the opportunity to experience leadership, learn skills in your career area, and have fun with other students interested in marketing. The first round competitions will be held in January at the Gary Career Center, the state competitions in Indianapolis in February, and the National Conference in Anaheim, California, in April. As part of the learning experience, students will organize and run fund-raisers to help cover the costs of participating in the competitions.

Your first day in the Career Center is Tuesday, August 22. Our classroom is located on the second floor of the Career Center. We will meet Tuesdays from 12:45 pm to 1:30 pm and Wednesdays and Fridays from 11:30 am to 1:00 pm. We will not meet on Mondays and Thursdays.

I have sent to your parent or guardian an overview of the Marketing Education Program at Macon County Career Center and the "Network and Internet Access Agreement for Students." Please read the information and return the two forms with your and your parent's or guardian's signatures. The information includes a program description, the course outline, and a detailed description of the grading system. The grading system is based on a mastery approach to learning. The mastery system provides the opportunity for every student to master all the course content.

Fees include $30 for textbook rental and supplies and $15 for DECA (local and national) membership. If you pay by check, please make two separate checks, each payable to Macon County Career and Technical Center. You can bring the payments to school, or you can send them to the Career Center.

If you have any questions or concerns, please contact me at the Career Center, 555-555-0170, or my home, 555-555-0197.

Judy Commers

Mrs. Judy Commers
Marketing Foundations Teacher

Figure H-3. Student Letter. Notice the enthusiasm conveyed in the first paragraph and the key information provided, including how to contact the teacher.

Marketing Class Seating Chart

_______ Period

	Row 1	Row 2	Row 3	Row 4	Row 5	Row 6
Seat 5						
Seat 4						
Seat 3						
Seat 2						
Seat 1						

Front of Classroom

Figure H-4. Seating Chart. This is a typical seating chart. You may reproduce this one for use in your classes.

Seat Assignments

Cut slips apart and write in the seat assignments. If possible, laminate for durability. Place slips in an envelope or bowl, and have students take seat assignments as they enter the room.

Welcome to Marketing! Your seat is Row ___, Seat ___	Welcome to Marketing! Your seat is Row ___, Seat ___	Welcome to Marketing! Your seat is Row ___, Seat ___
Welcome to Marketing! Your seat is Row ___, Seat ___	Welcome to Marketing! Your seat is Row ___, Seat ___	Welcome to Marketing! Your seat is Row ___, Seat ___
Welcome to Marketing! Your seat is Row ___, Seat ___	Welcome to Marketing! Your seat is Row ___, Seat ___	Welcome to Marketing! Your seat is Row ___, Seat ___
Welcome to Marketing! Your seat is Row ___, Seat ___	Welcome to Marketing! Your seat is Row ___, Seat ___	Welcome to Marketing! Your seat is Row ___, Seat ___
Welcome to Marketing! Your seat is Row ___, Seat ___	Welcome to Marketing! Your seat is Row ___, Seat ___	Welcome to Marketing! Your seat is Row ___, Seat ___

Figure H-5. Seat Assignments. An easy and random way to assign seats is to create seat assignment slips, as shown in this figure. You can reproduce this page and fill in the seat assignments for your room. Laminating them will enable you to use them over and over again.

organizational tools you need in your classroom. How will you dispense and collect materials? How will you collect homework and project assignments, tests, and workbook sheets? How will you make sure that absent students receive handouts and homework assignments? For ideas and suggestions, see the third edition of *The First Days of School* by Harry and Rosemary Wong and "Dispensing Materials in Fifteen Seconds" by Harry and Rosemary Wong (http://teachers.net/gazette/SEP02/wong.html).

Develop a Classroom Management Plan

Successful sports teams have a game plan. Successful armies have a battle plan. Successful businesses have a business plan. Successful teachers have a classroom management plan.

What is a classroom management plan? It is a set of procedures and routines, developed by the teacher and taught to the students. Optimally, you should develop your classroom management plan before school starts. Optimally, you should have procedures and routines for all aspects of student behavior and activity in your classroom. Some teachers create a classroom management binder with reproducibles of the procedures and routines; others create electronic presentations to teach the procedures and routines to their students.

What types of topics should be covered in a classroom management plan? How to enter the classroom, what to do when you get to your seat ("bell work" or "warm-up activities"), how to get the class quiet, how to take attendance, how homework and classwork will be collected, what to do when you have been absent, how the class will be dismissed, and so on.

The First Five Minutes

One of the most critical aspects of classroom management is to have an orderly, consistent way to start the class. The first five minutes are critical. Your key responsibility at the start of class is to get the students working right away. Designate an area in the classroom—on the board, on an overhead transparency projected on the board, a bulletin board, a flip chart, or a handout placed on the desks—where students will look as soon as they sit down for the first activity of the class. These first activities are known as "bell ringer" or "warm-up" activities. You need to impress upon students that learning begins as soon as they enter

your classroom and sit down. Make the first few minutes as exciting and as important as possible. Generate the feeling that if they miss the first few minutes, they will have a hard time catching up. While students are working on the first activity, you can handle necessary administrative tasks such as taking attendance.

The *Marketing Dynamics* program provides many ideas for warm-up activities. You can assign a section of text, then have students write their answers to the "Reality Check" question. You can assign questions from the "Review Concepts" and "Think Critically" sections of the Chapter Review. (Notice that the *Teacher's Edition* has an annotation titled "Review It Now." This annotation suggests specific chapter review questions to assign after brief sections of text.) You can assign worksheets from the *Student Workbook.* You can use activity suggestions in the annotations of the *Teacher's Edition* and in the teaching strategies in the *Teacher's Resources.* In addition, the *Activity Buffet* in this handbook has a section, "Warm-Ups," which has a variety of additional suggestions.

Rules

Classroom rules are a necessary foundation for student learning. Rules should be introduced and taught at the beginning of the school year. Teachers vary in how they develop their rules. Some have a set of rules that they post in the classroom, distribute to students and their parents, and teach and review throughout the school year. Other teachers have the students develop the rules, then post, distribute, and teach them throughout the school year. Some teachers like to call their rules "Rules and Responsibilities," to emphasize the students' responsibilities.

Rules can be as simple or as complex as you wish. Some teachers find the golden rule, "Do unto others as you would have done unto you," to be sufficient. Others have three brief rules: (1) Enter class quietly. (2) Only one person speaks at a time. (3) Respect everyone and their property. Others have success with a more detailed list of rules. Use what works best for you.

Establish an Atmosphere of Respect

How will you establish an atmosphere of respect? One of the main ways is for you, the teacher, to model respectful behavior. Treat yourself with respect and dignity. Dress and act like a professional every day. Every day, greet each student with enthusiasm as he or she enters your classroom. Acknowledge students when you pass them in the hall. Treat others with respect. Never criticize anyone in public, and do not allow students to criticize or "put down" others. When a student speaks, give him or her all your attention, and make sure the rest of the class does, too.

Especially in a large school and large classes, it is often difficult to connect with each student. However, acknowledging and connecting with someone is a sign of respect. That is why it is important to acknowledge your students when you pass them in the hall, to give each student full attention when he or she speaks in class, and to make time for one-on-one interactions. For a student who is shy in class or disinclined to hang out for a few minutes to talk with you, try talking with him or her while walking somewhere. The side-by-side dynamic and the physical aspect of walking often set the stage for a more comfortable interaction.

Be a "good finder." In other words, notice what your students do that is good, and acknowledge it. You might post students' good activities on a bulletin board. Good activities can include everything from helping another student, to volunteer work in the community, to athletic and scholastic accomplishments. In the day-to-day interaction with students, let them know how proud you are of them. Make positive observations and comments to each student as often as you can. Make sure that you include all students and leave no one out. Work especially hard to find good things about your problem, difficult, or struggling students.

Send a note to parents when students do something good. Usually, parents are only contacted when there are problems, and such notes or calls home often trigger conflict between parents and their student. Contact parents when their student does something good, especially if the student has been having difficulties. In this situation, the positive feedback could very well trigger positive interactions between the parents and their student.

As part of your "good finding," set up a system of certificates. Many word-processing programs have certificate forms that are easy to customize. Award certificates for projects and community service activities. Try to set up the certificate system so that each student can possibly get a certificate for something, but do not make obtaining a certificate so simple that the certificate seems worthless. See also the section "Using Rewards in the Classroom," page 37.

Acknowledge each student's birthday. One way is to include a "happy birthday" note on each student's birth date on the class calendar. You might place a birthday card on the student's desk on the day of his or her birthday. If it is not too disruptive, announce the birthday and have the class sing "happy birthday."

Establish an Atmosphere of Friendliness and Warmth

Smile. We all smile, no matter what language we speak. A smile usually conveys friendliness, warmth, and happiness. Have your students try an experiment. Have them smile whenever they pass someone in the hall at school or at the mall. Have them smile at customers at work, family members at home, and people who wait on them when they are the customers. What is the reaction of the person they smiled at? Did the person smile back? How did the student feel when he or she smiled at someone? Did making a point of smiling at others make them feel happier?

As a teacher, you may have realized that when you see smiling faces looking at you, it is more fun to teach. Suggest to your students that they try the smiling experiment on you. You might just start a mutually smiling environment that is a welcoming place to be!

Use humor in your classroom, as appropriate. Use humorous cartoons on handouts, bulletin boards, and electronic presentations. If you make a mistake, laugh at yourself so students can see that we all make errors. Teach students how to laugh *with* someone, not *at* them. Never make fun of a student or allow students to make fun of each other.

The Last Five Minutes

The last five minutes of class should be as calm and orderly as the first five minutes. Make sure students know that *you* dismiss the class, not a bell, the clock, or other students. At the same time, you should plan your classes so that you allow enough time at the end for closure for the activity, to make any last minute announcements or assignments, and for students to clean up and pack up their belongings. If you have an extra minute or two before the bell rings, and students are ready to leave, make sure that they stay seated. Suggest that they relax, perhaps close their eyes, and review what they have accomplished today and what they yet need to accomplish.

Facilitate Self-Management

By providing students with procedures and routines, you enable students to manage themselves and take responsibility for their learning. Also see "Strategies for Effective Teaching: Mastery Learning," pages 23–24, for some specific suggestions that enable students to manage their learning.

Successful self-management will lead students to better accomplishments in their schoolwork and to higher self-esteem.

The First Day

Last but not least! After you have done most of your planning, plan the first day. As many marketing and human resources researchers have observed, you have less than a minute to make a good first impression; and, sometimes unfortunately, the first impression is the lasting impression. Many educators have observed that the first day of school sets the tone for the whole school year. For these reasons, the first day of school is critical.

Many teachers report that they have more success on the first day if they plan a script to follow and have each class planned to the minute. The following are some suggestions to think about as you plan your first day.

The Classroom

Refer back to the section "Prepare Your Classroom." Make sure your posters and displays are ready. Have the title of the course, course number (if used), class meeting times, and your name prominently posted. Have the seating charts and the envelope of seat assignments on a desk near the door, so students can take one of each as they enter the class.

Greeting Students

Keep in mind that the students are just as nervous as you are! Stand out in the hallway near your door. Greet students with a smile and a handshake. You might say, "Hi! Are you looking for Marketing?" Then if they are not in marketing, you have given them the opportunity to find the right classroom for the class they are enrolled in for this hour.

If they are in marketing this hour, introduce yourself and ask them their names. Try to remember their names and pronunciations. Tell them to take a seating chart, take a seat assign-ment from the envelope, and find their seats. After thay have found their seats, ask them to pass the seat assignment slips forward for the next class.

Introductions

After attendance has been taken, welcome everyone to your class and begin by introducing yourself. Tell them information about yourself, for example, "I received my bachelor's degree in marketing from the University of Texas and my Master's in Teaching from Michigan State. I have been teaching marketing for five years. This is my second year at your school. Previously, I taught at Central High School in Wisconsin." You might also want to show them your teaching certificate and explain what it means. It is up to you whether you want to share any personal information.

After you have introduced yourself, do this simple "Getting to Know You" activity. Have students get into pairs. If there is one student left over, that student is your partner. Tell students that the goal is to have each person introduce his or her partner, so that we can learn something about our classmates and write their names on our seating charts. They are to learn and share the following information about their partners: full name, nickname or preferred name (if appropriate), where they work if they work, which grade they are in (if it is a multi-grade class), what school they are from (if it is a center with students from several schools), and a hobby or favorite book, movie, song, or band. Give students about four minutes, two apiece, to learn the information.

Have each student introduce his or her partner. If you have partnered with someone, you and your partner should go first. Write the name and preferred name of each student on your overhead seating chart. Have students do the same on their copies of the seating chart.

After this activity is completed, distribute two 3x5 cards to each student. Ask students to write the following information on each card: their full name, preferred name, address (street, city, state, zip code), area code and phone number, date of birth, name of employer and employer location (if they work), career interest or plans, and their parents or guardians' names. You might also ask them to provide their parents' e-mail addresses.

While students are completing the cards, explain that one card will be kept at school and the other one will be kept at home. Their birthdays will be added to the class calendars. The parent and home information will be used if you need to contact their parents. Explain also that you often get requests for workers from area employers. Now that you have information about their career interests, you would be able to discuss employment opportunities with them and to recommend them to appropriate employers.

First Assignment

If you have displayed their names around the classroom, your first writing assignment can be to ask students to write one or two paragraphs that answer this question, "Why do you think I took the time to cut out the stars (or diamonds/sailboats/ etc.), put your names on them, laminate them, and hang them from the ceiling?" You might want students to do this as homework, due the next day. This might also be a good time to explain to students what you expect in a written assignment. Include your requirements for headers or title page and other format requirements. Emphasize that spelling and grammar count because spelling and grammar count in the work world.

You might be surprised by the responses to the question. There are no wrong answers. The purpose of this exercise is to see the students' writing ability and how creative they might be. Here are some samples of the types of responses you might get: to get us to learn each other's names, because you care about us, you wanted to make us feel welcome, you think we are shining stars, you think we are diamonds in the rough, because you want us to be DECA members and the diamond is their emblem, you want us to sail through this class, you just wanted to decorate the room with our names.

Another excellent first assignment is to have students write their autobiographies. It is a good way for you to learn about your students. Either assignment is a good way to find out about the students' writing abilities (or lack thereof).

After you have collected the assignment, read them over and choose several to read to the class and/or post on a bulletin board. For the autobiographies, get the student's permission before reading or posting.

Strategies for Effective Teaching

The *Marketing Dynamics* program is filled with specific teaching suggestions and strategies.

The following discussions present general strategies and approaches to teaching and learning and show how *Marketing Dynamics* supports these approaches.

Teaching the Millennials

Whether you are a seasoned marketing instructor or a new teacher, you need to understand the characteristics of the current generation of students. Called the "Millennials," students in this generation were born between 1982 and 2002. It is the largest generation, even surpassing the Baby Boomers. Here are some of their common traits:

- They can manipulate technology better then any previous generation.
- They are generally very confident.
- They have very short attention spans.
- They like to be busy and are excellent at multitasking. (They can be working on a computer, talking on a cell phone, and listening to music all at the same time and seem to be able to concentrate on all.)
- They are the most affluent and best-educated generation.
- They need to be engaged and very active in their learning.
- They like to congregate.
- They like being part of a team because it lowers the pressure on them as individuals.
- They expect projects to be highly structured.
- They need to be held accountable.
- They are the most tested generation.
- They have been pressured to perform and pushed by their Boomer parents to be the best they can be.
- They are also very close to their parents, as evidenced by their frequent contact by cell phone. They tend to discuss things with their parents.
- These students and their parents strive for recognition.
- They get excited about applying education to the real world, and they want to know what the topic/lesson has to do with them.

- They are the first generation that received awards not just for winning, but also for participation.

Of course, these are generalizations, and each student is an individual with unique traits and life experiences. However, your awareness of these traits will help you develop lessons that will be more appealing to this generation.

Here are some general suggestions for teaching this generation. (See also the sections that follow for more detailed teaching strategies.) Set rules and expectations from the very beginning, and give them to students in writing. Let students also know from the beginning how they will be graded and when testing will occur. Include a syllabus. A monthly calendar, with content coverage and testing dates is very beneficial. See Figure H-1 and the discussion of curriculum planning.

These students are close with their parents, so communicate with the parents. Send them a letter before school starts, describing the course. See sample parent letter, Figure H-2. When their student has accomplished something, let the parents know in a note or letter. Plan events in which parents can participate or observe. Consider establishing a Web page or blog where parents (and students) can go to learn what is happening in class, what assignments are due, and what special events are planned.

Since these students want to know how the topics they are studying will be useful to them, be sure to address this issue in your teaching. One prereading activity for each part (in the *Teacher's Edition*) asks students to predict what they will learn and how it would be useful to a marketer. The annotations "Workplace Connection" and the Chapter Review sections "Connect to Business" and "Explore Careers" help students connect what they are learning to the business world and their potential future careers.

These students like to be involved and active in their learning. *Marketing Dynamics* provides many activities to meet this need. The Part Opener Activities, found in the Teacher's Resources, provide hands-on, minds-on activities that use many learning modalities. These activities are an excellent way to get all students involved in their learning. Role plays are another excellent way to get students involved. Eighteen official DECA role plays, two per part, are provided in the Teacher's Resources. In addition, the *Activity Buffet—Role Plays* (in this *Handbook*) provides guidelines for making up your own role plays. In addition, the

Teacher's Edition annotations and the *Teacher's Resources* "Chapter Teaching Strategies" provide hundreds of activity ideas.

Another way for students to be involved and responsible for their learning is through "mastery learning." See the section "Mastery Learning."

This generation enjoys doing things in groups. Many of the activity suggestions in the *Marketing Dynamics* program are for "cooperative learning." See the section "Cooperative Learning."

Teaching is a dynamic and challenging task. The *Marketing Dynamics* program provides many specific teaching suggestions and aids to make teaching easier and more fun. The following sections provide some guidance in general teaching strategies.

Overview of Teaching Approaches

You can make your classroom exciting and relevant by using a variety of teaching approaches. Here is an overview of approaches.

Make Learning Stimulating

One way to do this is to involve students in lesson planning. When possible, allow them to select the modes of learning they enjoy most. For example, some students will do well with oral reports; others prefer written assignments. Some learn well through group projects; others do better working independently. You can also make the class more interesting by presenting a variety of learning activities and projects, then allowing students to choose the one that interests them the most to fulfill their requirements. The *Marketing Dynamics Teacher's Edition* and the *Teacher's Resources* provide many suggestions for activities and projects.

Make Learning Realistic

You can make learning realistic by relating the subject matter to situations with which the students are familiar. The student text does this by using concrete and familiar examples to present and explain concepts. The "Reality Check" features in the student text ask students to apply what they just learned to their own lives and experiences. Also in the student text, the Chapter Review sections "Connect to Business," "Explore Careers," and "Connect to the Internet" give students opportunities to apply marketing concepts to the real world and their own lives.

Take advantage of the students who work. Use the "Workplace Connection" annotations in the *Teacher's Edition* as a basis to get student-workers to share their marketing-relevant experiences. The supervisors of these student-workers might also be an excellent source for real world experiences.

Take students out to the real world, or invite the real world in to your students. Because marketing is everywhere in our society, have students do outside-of-school projects that require them to observe in local stores and malls, watch TV, observe local traffic, and/or visit a local bank. You can also bring the real world to your students through speakers, newspapers and magazines, videos, the Internet, and telephone and business directories. Many ideas for these sorts of activities appear in the *Teacher's Edition* and *Teacher's Resources*. Each chapter in the *Teacher's Resources* has a section on "Speakers and Field Trips."

Role plays are another excellent way to bring marketing concepts to life. Official DECA role plays, two per part, are provided in the *Teacher's Resources*. In addition, you and the students can create your own role plays for most topics. Guidelines and worksheets for developing your own role plays are in the *Activity Buffet —Role Plays*.

Make Learning Varied

If you generally stand in front of the class and lecture, think about using different methods to present concepts. The *Marketing Dynamics* program provides a wealth of activities to add variety to your teaching. Variety in presentation is especially important when you have block scheduling. See sections "Cooperative Learning," "How to Structure a Class Session (including Block Scheduling)," and "How to Manage Activities in the Classroom."

Make Learning Success-Oriented

Help students experience success in your class. Experiencing success increases self-esteem and confidence. Guarantee success for students by presenting a variety of learning activities. Key these activities to different ability levels so each student can enjoy both success and challenge. You will also want to allow for individual learning styles and talents. For instance, some students excel at organizing material, whereas others are artistic or analytical. Build in opportunities for individual students to work in ways and at projects that let them succeed and shine.

Another way to increase success is to implement a mastery approach to learning. See the section "Mastery Learning."

Make Learning Personal

Young people become more personally involved in learning if you establish a comfortable rapport with them. Work toward a relaxed classroom atmosphere in which students can feel at ease when sharing their feelings and ideas in group discussions and activities.

The "Reality Check" feature in the student text helps students apply the concepts learned to their personal lives or to the world around them. The "Journal Writing" annotation in the *Teacher's Edition* also encourages students to think about their personal responses to their learning.

Learning also becomes more personal if students can pursue topics that they are interested in. Students generally become more interested in a class and less disruptive when the course content relates to something they are interested in. Find out what students are interested in and draw examples from that area. Examples from sports and entertainment often engage students' interest. To the extent possible, let students choose their own topics for projects, news article reports, and so on. For example, you might have a student who is usually disruptive and does not want to be in school. However, when you discover that he is interested in race cars and racing, you encourage him to read and report to the class about marketing and racing. Such a student might surprise you by settling down, participating in class, and learning a great deal.

Help students find what they are most interested in, what excites them, what area they might want to pursue for their careers. Encourage them to set their goals and to dream about their futures. Show you care, and students will probably be excited about the class and not create discipline problems in your classroom. Keep in mind the old saying, "Students won't care until they know you care."

However, while making learning personal, you must also respect students' right to privacy. Some activities, such as autobiographies, journals, and opinion papers may violate students' rights to privacy. You can maintain confidentiality by letting students turn in unsigned papers in these situations. You may also encourage students to pursue some of these activities at home for personal enlightenment without fear of evaluation or judgment.

Communicating with Students

Teaching is communicating. Communicating with high school students is often challenging. Communicating with students involves not only sending clear messages but also receiving and interpreting feedback. Through the way you communicate with students, you can establish that warm and relaxed classroom atmosphere that encourages participation.

- **Use body language effectively.** Recognize the importance of body language and nonverbal communication, both in presenting material and in interpreting students' responses. Use eye contact, a relaxed but attentive body posture, natural gestures, and an alert facial expression. Wear a genuine smile. Look for the same body language from students to indicate their level of attention.

- **Voice is also an important nonverbal communicator.** Cultivate a warm, lively, enthusiastic speaking voice, especially when making presentations. By your tone, you can convey a sense of acceptance and expectation to which your students will respond.

- **Create a nonjudgmental atmosphere.** Students will only communicate freely and participate in classroom activities if the environment is comfortable. You can make students comfortable by respecting their ideas, by accepting them for who they are, and by honoring their confidences. It is also important to avoid criticizing a student or discussing a student's personal matters in front of others.

- **Share some of your feelings and experiences.** The measure of what students communicate to you may depend in part on what you are willing to share with them. Describe your personal experiences, ideas, and feelings as appropriate. However, the classroom is *not* a forum for you to promulgate a political, religious, or lifestyle point of view. It is also *not* a place for you to "let it all hang out" or vent about your feelings or life problems. Be judicious in what you share with students, but do share some of yourself, especially your enthusiasm. Also tell students about a few of your mistakes.

Sharing will initiate exchange and start building a relationship between you and the students.

- **Use humor whenever possible.** Humor is not only good medicine, it also opens doors and teaches lasting lessons. Laughter will reduce tension, make points in a nonthreatening and memorable way, increase the fun and pleasure in classroom learning, and break down stubborn barriers. Relevant cartoons, quotations, jokes, and amusing stories all bring a light touch to the classroom.

- **Listen.** Listen for what students say, what they mean, and what they do not say. Really listening may be the single most important step you can take to promote open communication. As students answer questions and express their ideas and concerns, try not only to hear what they say, but also to understand what they mean. What students leave unsaid can be as important as what they do say.

- **Ask questions.** Good questions are tools that open the door to communication. Ask questions that promote recall, discussion, and thought. Use the following open-ended questions to stimulate thoughtful answers: what, where, why, when, and how. You can draw out students by asking for their opinions and conclusions. The "Reality Checks" in the student text, annotations in the *Teacher's Edition*, and the strategies in the *Teacher's Resources* contain many discussion questions. Avoid questions with yes or no answers, as they tend to discourage rather than promote further communication. Avoid questions that are too personal or that might put students on the spot. Allow time for silence and time to think and reflect during discussion sessions.

- **Rephrase students' responses.** Paraphrasing students' answers and comments is a great way to clarify, refine, and reinforce ideas under discussion. For example, you might say, "This is what I hear you saying…Correct me if I'm wrong." Positive acknowledgment of students' contributions, insights, and successes encourages more active participation and open communication. Try such comments as: "That's a very good point. I hadn't thought of it that way before." "What a great idea!"

- **Use written communication to advantage.** Very often, the written word can be an excellent way to connect. Written messages can take different forms, for example, a note on the board, a note attached to homework or other assignment, a memo to parents (with good news as well as bad), or a letter exchange involving class members.

- **Be open and available for private discussions.** It is important to let students know they can come to you with personal concerns as well as questions regarding course material. You need to handle these discussions and disciplinary actions confidentially and usually in a private setting. If you have trouble connecting with a student, you might try the "walk and talk" approach; that is, find a time when you can walk alongside the student as he or she is on the way down the hall or to the parking lot. Walking and talking relieves some of the pressure of a direct approach or confrontation, and can be a helpful setting for initiating communication with a student.

Helping Students Value Diversity

Your students will be entering a rapidly changing workplace—not only in the area of technology, but also in the diverse nature of its workforce. Years ago, the workforce was dominated by white males, but 85 percent of the new entrants into the workforce now are women, minorities, and immigrants. The workforce is also aging. Over half of the workforce will be people between the ages of 35 and 54. Because of these changes, young workers will need to be able to interact effectively with those who are different from themselves.

The appreciation and understanding of diversity is an ongoing process. The earlier and more frequently young people are exposed to diversity, the better able they will be to bridge cultural differences. If your students are exposed to different cultures within your classroom, they can begin the process of understanding cultural differences. This is the best preparation for success in a diverse society. In addition, teachers have found the following strategies to be helpful:

- Actively promote a spirit of openness, consideration, respect, and tolerance in your classroom.

- Use a variety of teaching styles and assessment strategies.

- Use cooperative learning activities whenever possible. Make sure group roles are rotated so everyone has leadership opportunities.

- When grouping students, make sure the composition of each group is as diverse as possible with regard to gender, race, and nationality. If the groups present information to the class, make sure all members have a speaking part.

- Make sure one culture's opinions are not over-represented during class discussions. Seek opinions of under-represented persons or cultures as appropriate.

- If a student makes a sexist, racist, or otherwise offensive comment, ask the student to rephrase the comment in a manner that will not offend other members of the class. Remind students that offensive statements and behavior are inappropriate in the workplace as well as the classroom.

- If a difficult classroom situation arises based on a diversity issue, ask for a time-out and have everyone write down his or her thoughts and opinions about the incident. This allows everyone to cool down and allows you to plan a response.

- Arrange for guest speakers who represent diversity in gender, race, and ethnicity even though the topic does not relate to diversity.

- Have students change seats from time to time throughout the course, so that they have the opportunity to sit next to people they do not know well.

- Several times during the course, have students do anonymous evaluations of the class. Specifically ask them to mention any problems that they would like to share with you.

- Provide students with experiences to interact with people significantly older than they are. Many future job opportunities will involve working with aging Baby Boomers and senior citizens. Perhaps you can set up service activities in local retirement or nursing homes. Suggestions for these types of activities appear in the *Teacher's Edition* and in the *Teacher's Resources*.

Developing Critical Thinking Skills

When today's students graduate and leave their classrooms behind, they will face a world of complexity and change. Over their lifetimes, they are likely to work in several career areas and hold many different jobs. Providing young people with a base of knowledge consisting only of facts, principles, and procedures will be doing them a disservice. They must, in addition, be prepared to solve complex problems, make difficult decisions, and assess ethical implications. In other words, students must be able to use critical thinking skills. These skills are often referred to as the higher-order thinking skills. Benjamin Bloom listed these as

- **Analysis**—breaking down material into its component parts so its organizational structure may be understood.
- **Synthesis**—putting parts together to form a new whole.
- **Evaluation**—judging the value of material for a given purpose.

In a broader perspective, students must be able to use reflective thinking in order to decide what to believe and do. According to Robert Ennis, students should be able to

- Define and clarify problems, issues, conclusions, reasons, and assumptions.
- Judge the credibility, relevance, and consistency of information.
- Infer or solve problems and draw reasonable conclusions.

Modeling Critical Thinking

One of the unique aspects of *Marketing Dynamics* is that the student text models critical thinking. Most texts have critical thinking activities, such as review questions, activities, and tests. *Marketing Dynamics* has all of these. However, students often have no experience thinking critically and do not know how to do it. To help them, the *Marketing Dynamics* student text models critical thinking. Modeling critical thinking means showing the process of thinking and problem solving. In other words, you show how one gets from thought *A* to thought *D* by showing thoughts *B* and *C*. Critical thinking also involves knowing what questions to ask.

Marketing Dynamics models critical thinking by asking questions in the text, then showing how the questions are answered. Questions appear throughout the text, and the critical thinking is shown in the following text, for example, on text page 244, "Is Marketing Research Always Right?" and page 277, "What Is a 'New' Product?" Critical thinking is also modeled when the text explains how to interpret tables and graphs, for example on text pages 231–232, where Figure 19-9 is discussed.

In the student text, the "Reality Checks" and the "Think Critically" section of the "Chapter Review" are designed to challenge students to think critically. The annotations "Critical Thinking" in the *Teacher's Edition* and the "Discuss" questions in the *Teacher's Resources* are also designed to get the students to think critically.

Role Plays

Role plays provide an excellent opportunity for practicing critical thinking. Role plays challenge students to solve problems, apply their knowledge, and think creatively. Role playing allows students to practice solving problems and making decisions under nonthreatening circumstances. It also enables students to examine the feelings of others as well as their own. Such activities can help students learn effective ways to react or cope when confronted with similar situations in their own work lives. Official DECA role plays are provided in the *Teacher's Resources*, and guidelines for developing your own role plays are provided in the *Activity Buffet— Role Plays*.

Brainstorming

Another type of activity that develops creativity and can be used to develop critical thinking skills is brainstorming. Many of the activities suggest brainstorming. Brainstorming is a process of collecting as many ideas on a particular topic as possible, without judging any of them. The concept is to collect the ideas first, then work with them. Brainstorming can be done with the whole class, but is often more effective when done first by small groups, then each group's results are collected.

Each group gets a large piece of butcher paper (or a large pad on an easel) and a marker. The paper can be taped to a wall. One person is the recorder. The group is given a topic on which to brainstorm, such as names of local businesses. If the group has enough self-discipline, let each person shout out a name. The recorder then writes it down on the paper. If the group is not disciplined, then each person gets a turn to name a business. The recorder keeps recording until the group has run out of ideas. These lists can then be used for grouping/categorizing and other activities.

Debate

Debate is an excellent way to explore opposite sides of an issue. You may want to divide the class into two groups, each to take an opposing side of the issue. You can also ask students to work in smaller groups and explore opposing sides of an issue. Each group can select students from the group to present the points for their side. Suggestions for debate topics are in the "Chapter Teaching Strategies" section of the *Teacher's Resources*.

Turning Your Class into a Team

Business emphasizes teamwork, so we do our students a favor by teaching them how to work in teams. The text presents concepts of interpersonal skills and teamwork in Chapter 51, but you can start developing teamwork from the first day of class.

The first step in an effective team is helping the team members feel comfortable with each other. This can be achieved through activities that help students get to know each other, such as the introduction activity on the first day. The *Activity Buffet—Getting to Know You* provides additional activities.

Many of the activities in the *Marketing Dynamics* program can be carried out in teams, especially the DECA role plays, Part Opener Activities, and "Cooperative Learning" activities in the *Teacher's Edition* and the *Teacher's Resources*. One of the keys to successful team activities is to make sure that the team knows the goal or objective of the activity. Before you start a team activity, you might ask someone in the class to state the objective of the activity and have all students write it down. Another activity could be having your whole class consider themselves a team or a business, and have them develop a class mission statement.

Cooperative Learning

Because of the emphasis on teamwork in the workplace, the use of cooperative learning groups in your classroom will give students an opportunity to practice teamwork skills. During cooperative learning, students learn interpersonal and small-group skills that will allow them to function as part of a team. These skills include leadership, decision making, trust building, communication, and conflict management.

The cooperative activities in *Marketing Dynamics* usually begin with the words, "organize students into groups or teams." There are many ways to organize students into groups. However you set up your groups, it is advisable to vary the composition of the groups periodically to give students the opportunity to work with a variety of different classmates. At least some of the time, groups should be mixed in terms of abilities and talents so there are opportunities for the students to learn from one another. In addition, as groups work together over time, the roles should be rotated so everyone has an opportunity to practice and develop different skills. Some of the team activities in *Marketing Dynamics* are related and build on each other; for these activities, it might be a good idea to keep the same team composition.

With cooperative learning, students learn to work together toward a group goal. Each member is dependent on others for the outcome. This interdependence is a basic component of any cooperative learning group or work team. Students understand that one person cannot succeed unless everyone succeeds. The value of each group member is affirmed as learners work toward the group goal. This is true in business also. Everyone in the business, from the president to the maintenance staff, has critical work to do. Each person individually and as part of the group must perform to his or her best so that the business can meet its goal. This idea is also part of the marketing concept: everyone in the company must work together to satisfy customer needs and wants. If your students are involved in a school-based enterprise, they will see this in action in their school store or other business.

Another value of using cooperative groups is that it gives more students a chance to participate. If you have a whole-class discussion, usually only three to five students speak. If you organize the class into cooperative groups of three to five, each student will have a chance to speak. Students are also less likely to feel intimidated if speaking to a smaller group, rather than the whole class. In a cooperative group, students are more likely to share their ideas and take the risk to participate. To hear everyone's ideas or results, each group can elect someone to present the group's ideas or results to the class. Monitor the groups to make sure that everyone gets a chance to present ideas and results.

You will need to monitor the effectiveness of the groups, intervening as necessary to provide task assistance or to help with interpersonal and group skills. At the conclusion of group activities, evaluate students' achievement and help them discuss how well they collaborated with each other and what they can do to improve their interactions the next time they work in a group. You might have groups fill out the "Participation Evaluation: Team" form in the *Activity Buffet— Communication.*

Mastery Learning

Many marketing teachers find "mastery learning" to be a valuable approach to teaching marketing. The structure of the *Marketing Dynamics* program lends itself particularly well to this approach to teaching and learning.

What Is Mastery Learning?

Mastery learning is an approach to teaching and learning that says that all students can learn, provided that they are given appropriate instruction and time to learn. There are many sources for information on the mastery learning approach; but in short, the following are some of its key characteristics:

- Subject matter is organized into small portions.
- Objectives for each portion state specifically what students must master for each portion.
- Testing covers objectives. In other words, students know exactly what they need to study and master for the test.
- Testing is used to assess mastery and as a guide to help students master what they do not know.
- Additional activities are provided to students who need more help to master the objectives.
- Students are allowed to take the time they need to master objectives.
- Students are given more than one opportunity to show mastery.

- Students must master a minimum number of objectives before they can progress to the next portion.
- Learning is often enhanced because students are given responsibility and control over their level of learning.

Applying Mastery Learning

The *Marketing Dynamics* program makes it easy for you to implement mastery learning. The chapters are short and focus on a few key concepts and terms, presented on the first page of each chapter. The "Remember This" section in the "Chapter Review" of each chapter summarizes the key concepts of the chapter.

The curriculum planning process, described on pages 5–6, works particularly well in the mastery learning environment. This process uses the National Standards Performance Indicators as objectives. These objectives are assigned (during your planning process) to dates on which they will be presented in class and dates on which they will be tested. See the sample calendar, Figure H-1. Students know ahead of time what content will be covered and when, and when they must know it for a test.

Tests are structured so that a student must receive 80 percent to show mastery of the required objectives. If students do not get 80 percent, they are given the opportunity to study some more and take another test on the same material. The *Marketing Dynamics* program provides many activities to help students learn, relearn, and reinforce what they have learned. In addition to the many activities in the *Student Workbook, Teacher's Edition,* and *Teacher's Resources,* the *Activity Buffet* categories of *Assessment, Content Review, Games,* and *Vocabulary* provide a wealth of generic activities that can be used to review and reinforce concepts, objectives, and performance indicators.

The mastery approach requires that you have several versions of tests that cover the same material. The **Exam***View*® *Assessment Suite CD* enables you to make many versions of tests on the same content.

This system of requiring a minimum grade for mastery enables most students to learn the basics, if they just work hard enough. This system gives them more than one chance to learn the material.

A Point Grading System

The mastery approach is often coupled with a point grading system. This point grading system specifies how many points are required for each letter grade. For example, a C might be 400 points, while an A is 600 points. The students are given the point grading system at the beginning of the semester, along with what needs to be done to achieve the requisite points. Usually, the additional points for Bs and As come from projects or activities for which the students can choose from a wide array of topics. This choice enables students to do creative and in-depth work on subjects of particular interest to themselves, rather than on a topic chosen by the teacher.

Students know how much work it takes to get each grade. Students can decide at the beginning of the semester what grade they want, and can then plan their studies and projects to achieve that grade. In this system, everyone can get an A if he or she works for it. This approach gives students more responsibility as well as control over their grades. This system often inspires students to work harder and achieve better grades. See Figure H-6 for a sample point system and Figure H-7 for a sample description of how points can be earned.

In addition, a flexible points system enables students to keep their grades up if they do poorly on one test or assignment. To make up for that low score, students can do extra projects or activities and earn extra points to make up for the points lost from doing poorly on a test or assignment. Figure H-8 shows guidelines for the class notebook, which can be graded for extra points. Grading the notebook for extra points is one way to teach and encourage students to keep an organized notebook.

Student Days

An important element of mastery learning is time to take tests and time for students to retake tests as necessary. One way to allow for this is to establish student days. A *student day* is a day on which tests and quizzes are given. On student days when tests and quizzes are not scheduled, students can retake tests and quizzes as needed or work on other projects and activities to earn additional points.

For example, you can establish Fridays as student days. On your calendar, you would indicate the schedule of tests and quizzes, and what objectives or performance indicators will be covered on each test or quiz. See Figure H-1. You would also give each student guidelines on what to do on student days. See Figure H-9. This system provides the necessary opportunity for students to retake tests and quizzes. It also provides time for students to work on projects and activities to earn additional points to raise their grades. If you instruct and monitor your students well enough, student days should go very smoothly, with each student pursuing what he or she needs to do. You can then circulate around the room, providing guidance as needed.

How to Structure a Class Session (including Block Scheduling)

Here are guidelines to keep in mind when you plan a lesson:

- Stick to your routine for the first and last five minutes.
- Establish one or more learning goals for the students.
- Use activities that enable students to achieve the goals.
- Help students construct their own knowledge.
- Vary the activities.
- Incorporate assessment.

How long it takes to accomplish goals or complete an activity in the classroom varies with the students and the course. Always have more material than you think you can cover. Be flexible. Have alternative approaches for difficult concepts. As you gain more experience teaching and managing the classroom, you will get a better idea of how long various activities usually take.

Stick to Your Established Routines

As described in "Develop a Classroom Management Plan," pages 13–15, it is very beneficial to establish a routine for starting and ending your class period. For each lesson or class meeting that you plan, determine how much time you have left for teaching after you subtract the first and last five minutes from the time period. Now you know how much time you have to work with for that lesson or class meeting.

Establish Learning Goals

When planning a lesson, the first step is to decide what the students should be able to do by the end of the class session. Many traditional

(Continued on page 29)

Point Grading System

You will determine your grade in this course based on the number of points you earn. Information on how to earn points is on a separate sheet, "How To Earn Points." This sheet shows you how many points are required for each letter grade.

This grading system treats you as a responsible adult. You can decide what grade you want and work toward it. If everyone decides to earn an A, that would be FANTASTIC!

Grading Scale

Refer to this table to find out the points required for each letter grade.

Grading Scale	
Letter Grade	**Point Range**
A+	784–800 or more
A	760–783
A–	728–759
B+	704–727
B	664–703
B–	640–663
C+	616–639
C	584–615
C–	560–583
D+	536–559
D	504–535
D–	480–503
F	479 or less

Allocation of Points

Refer to the chart below for the percentage and number of points that you can earn in each work category. You must earn at least the minimum number of points in each category. However, doing only the minimum will NOT earn you a passing grade. If you earn fewer than the minimum points in any category, you will not pass the course. Incompletes are given only in extreme cases. You must have all make-up work and test retakes completed by the last day of the semester.

Work Categories and Points				
Percentage of Grade	**Work Categories**	**Points**		
		Minimum	**Maximum**	**Extra Credit**
50%	Tests and Quizzes	240	400	0
15%	Professional Activities	80	120	30
10%	Written Work	50	80	10
10%	Work Ethic	25	80	0
5%	Career Specialization	20	40	20
5%	Current Events	30	40	10
5%	Portfolio	15	40	0
Bonus	Notebook	0	0	25
100%	**Total Work**	**460**	**800**	**95**

Figure H-6. Point Grading System. This is an example of the information sheet given to students to explain to them the point grading system.

How to Earn Points

Your grade in this class depends on how many points you earn. This sheet explains how you can earn points. Make sure you understand how points are earned for each category below. *If you miss a deadline for turning in work, you earn no points for the work.* However, you must still master the quiz or test content or turn in the work to earn a passing grade. See the separate sheet, "Points Grading System," to see how many points you need for each letter grade.

Tests and Quizzes (50% of grade): Quizzes will be given weekly and part tests at the end of each part. You must get 80 percent or better on a quiz or test to get any points. If you get 80 percent or better on your first try, you will get 50 points for a quiz and 100 points for a part test. If you get below 80 percent, you will get no points but will be given the opportunity to restudy and retake the quiz or test. If you get 80 percent or better on your second try, you will get 40 points for the quiz and 80 points for the part test. If three or more attempts are needed to get 80 percent, you will get 30 points for a quiz and 60 points for a test. *You must retake any quizzes or tests within five school days of your first attempt.* If five days or more pass before your second attempt, you can only receive 30 points for a quiz and 60 points for a test (when you get 80% or better).

Professional Activities (15% of grade): This category consists of points earned for participation in DECA–An Association of Marketing Students. You will receive points for attending DECA meetings, working on DECA community projects, and participating in conferences on your DECA activities. You can earn between 80 and 150 points for these activities. A separate list of activities and points will be provided to you.

Written Work (10% of grade): Each written assignment is worth 10 points. The minimum is five written assignments for 50 points. The standard is eight for 80 points. The maximum is nine for 90 points. A written assignment must be turned in within one week of the assignment date, or it will not be accepted.

Work Ethic (10% of grade): Between 25 and 80 points are awarded for attendance, attitude, and cooperation.

Career Specialization (5% of grade): This is an activity related to your career area. Activities are chosen from a list that will be provided to you. Each activity is worth 20 points. The minimum is one activity for 20 points. The standard is two activities for 40 points. The maximum is three activities for 60 points.

Current Events (5% of grade): This is a report written about a current event reported in a newspaper, magazine, or Internet news source. To receive credit, the report must answer the questions who, what, when, where, and why. Each current event report is worth 10 points. The minimum is three reports for 30 points. The standard is four reports for 40 points. The maximum is five reports for 50 points.

Portfolio (5% of grade): The portfolio is different from your class notebook (see below). The portfolio is a notebook of accomplishments for the semester, presented in a formal way. You will receive a separate sheet detailing what should be included and the points for each. You may receive between 15 and 40 points for your portfolio. It is due at the end of the grading period.

Notebook (bonus): If you wish an extra 5 to 25 bonus points, present your class notebook to your instructor at the end of the grading period. You will be given a separate sheet for what should be in your class notebooks and how they should be organized.

Figure H-7. How to Earn Points. This is an example of the information sheet given to students to explain to them what they need to do to earn points in each category of work.

Class Notebook Organization

If you wish, you may turn in your class notebooks for grading. The points you receive from the grading of your class notebooks are bonus points that will be added to your total points for the grading period. Turn in your class notebook to me at the end of the grading period.

Your class notebook contents should be in the order listed below. The papers should be three-hole punched, separated by tabs, and in a loose-leaf ring binder. Within each category, organize papers in date order. I will not grade a notebook that has papers falling out.

This class notebook is different from your portfolio. See separate guidelines for your portfolio. The portfolio is required. Turning in your class notebook is optional and is for bonus points.

Class Notebook Contents		
Section	**Title**	**Contents**
I	Assignments and Information	Assignment sheets, calendars, grading information, other informational handouts. (Note: Current calendar can be kept on the outside of your notebook.)
II	Tests and Quizzes	Keep all tests and quizzes that have been returned to you
III	Professional Activities	Keep all DECA information here
IV	Written Work	Keep all written work assignments that have been graded and returned to you
V	Career Specialization	Keep all career specialization activities that have been graded and returned to you
VI	Current Events	Keep all current events reports that have been graded and returned to you
VII	Portfolio	Keep all information and guidelines for portfolios here
VIII	Vocabulary	Keep all vocabulary activities here
IX	Notes	Keep any notes taken in class and while reading your text-book here

Figure H-8. Class Notebook Organization. This is an example of the information sheet given to students to explain to them how to organize their class notebooks. Many students need this kind of information, and some teachers award points as an incentive for students to keep a well-organized notebook.

Student Days

A student day is a day for you to take required tests and quizzes. When you finish the required tests and quizzes, you can use the time to work on marketing-related projects. The more marketing-related projects you finish, the more points you will earn, and the higher your grade will be. Follow the steps below for a successful student day!

Step 1	Take a quiz or test for the first time. If no test or quiz is assigned for today, go to step 2.
Step 2	Review for a quiz or test that you need to retake. When you are ready, go to step 3.
Step 3	Retake a quiz or test. When you have finished all your retakes, go to Step 4.
Step 4	After Step 3, you can do any one of the following: • Work on a written assignment for this class. • Read an article for your current events report, and write the report. • Work on a career specialization activity. • Work on a DECA activity or school store project.

WHAT <u>NOT</u> TO DO ON YOUR STUDENT DAY!

Do <u>not</u> do homework for another class.

Do <u>not</u> sleep.

Do <u>not</u> gossip or chat.

Do <u>not</u> use your phone.

Do <u>not</u> play games—paper or electronic.

Figure H-9. Student Days. This is an example of the information sheet given to students to explain to them what to do on a "student day."

lesson plans focus on what the teacher will do or the activities in which students will participate. Yet for learning (and after all, learning is the goal of school), you should focus on what you want students to be able to do.

If you have followed the guidelines in "Curriculum Planning Process" (pages 5–6), you have already designated which objectives you plan to cover on which days. Now all you have to do is structure your class activities around those objectives. If you are using the mastery approach, this first step of lesson planning fits right in. Since you have structured your course around the course objectives, you can now easily use those objectives to structure your class sessions.

Each chapter of the *Marketing Dynamics* student text starts with a list of objectives and key terms. The *Teacher's Edition* and the *Teacher's Resources* also provide a list of performance objectives from the *National Marketing and Business Administration Core Standards.* However, this list in itself is not sufficient. You must choose the objective(s) for each class period, then structure the students' learning experience so that they can accomplish the objective or objectives.

The number of objectives will depend on the difficulty of the objective, the learning ability of the students, and the length of time you have. Some objectives might take two or more class meetings each. Other objectives can be grouped together and accomplished in one class meeting.

The *Marketing Dynamics Teacher's Resource CD* contains a section of lesson plans. When you click on the link for "Lesson Plans," and a specific chapter, you see a customizable lesson plan form. Notice that all the objectives for the chapter are listed. That does not mean that you must "cover" all the objectives in one class meeting. You should look at these objectives and think about how best to help your students achieve them, then determine how much class time you want to spend on each one.

Use Activities

Lecturing is no longer the optimal way to help students learn. The attention span of most teens is very short. Many people think the attention span of students is correlated to their ages. For example, you can expect a 14-year-old to pay attention for 14 minutes; an 18-year-old, for 18 minutes. However, in general, 15 minutes should be the maximum amount of time that you expect students to sit still and concentrate on listening.

Five to ten minutes might be better. Lecturing time is best used to provide background for an activity or present a key concept.

You might ask, "If I'm not going to lecture, how am I going to present content?" First, keep in mind that your goal should *not* be "to present content." Your goal should be to provide ways for students to be able to accomplish objectives such as "List the Four Ps," "Distinguish between institutional and promotional advertising," "Describe the three retail approaches."

The way to help students achieve such goals is to create situations that require them to think about and use the information. You create such situations through activities. The *Marketing Dynamics* program provides a wealth of activities from which to choose. The student text provides "Reality Checks" and activities in the "Chapter Reviews." The *Student Workbook* provides worksheet activities to reinforce vocabulary and chapter concepts, as well as to review key math concepts. The *Teacher's Edition* provides a DECA cocurricular activity in the Lesson Planning Guide for each chapter and numerous activities in the wrap portion of each student page. The Teacher's Resources provide Part Opener Activities, DECA role plays, chapter teaching strategies, projects, and chapter tests. The *Activity Buffet* in this handbook provides a wealth of generic activities, suitable for use with all chapters and topics.

Your challenge as the teacher is to choose the activities that will best help your students master content and achieve the objectives.

Help Students Construct Knowledge

One of the goals of education is to help students "construct their own knowledge." What does this mean? It means that it is not enough to tell students what they need to know. It is not enough for students to read materials that they do not understand or do not remember. It means that the teacher must provide activities that lead students to think about what they are learning and to make the knowledge their own. In other words, teachers have to help students go through an invisible but critical process of absorbing and understanding new information.

When students have made knowledge their own, they do not memorize. They have added the knowledge in a way that they can use it and the knowledge becomes part of them. They have organized the knowledge in their own minds in a way that makes sense to them.

Lectures (short) and reading the text are a start. But the best way to help students construct their own knowledge is to involve them in activities. The *Marketing Dynamics* program provides many activities to help you do this. Key among the activities are the Part Opener Activities, found in the Teacher's Resources, one per part.

Activate Prior Knowledge. The first step in helping students construct their own knowledge is to provide them with a platform on which to build that knowledge. What is that platform? The knowledge that each student already has. You might say, "These students have never studied marketing before. What knowledge could they possibly have?" However, the philosophy of constructivist education says that each student knows something that can serve as a platform for building knowledge in a new area. The key is to bring out that knowledge that students already have. Once students are aware that they already know something about a subject, they feel good about themselves and their abilities to master the subject.

You are lucky that you are teaching marketing, because almost everyone in our society has had some experience with marketing, so it is relatively easy to bring out their knowledge. (However, good teachers in all subject areas figure out ways to bring out prior knowledge in their students because most students have some experience on which you can draw.)

The Part Opener Activities in the *Marketing Dynamics Teacher's Resources* are designed to activate the students' prior knowledge and provide a platform on which students can build further knowledge. These activities give students hands-on experiences and get them up and out of their seats and using many learning modalities and intelligences. The worksheets for each Part Opener Activity, provided in the *Teacher's Resources*, also include a few basic terms, which students can get familiar with before they start the part and chapters.

Provide Learning Experiences. Once you have activated students' prior knowledge, they are ready and usually eager to participate in more learning experiences. Suppose your objective for the class is "List the Four Ps." You might start out by having students search Chapter 1 and make their own list of the Four Ps. Not only does this get students thinking, but it also shows them that their textbook is a source of information. It is also an easy task that most students can do. Then have

students share what they found. You can then briefly lecture on the Four Ps. Then you can have students do another activity, such as creating a poster from ads to illustrate the Four Ps, having students cut out want ads and organizing them by the Four Ps, or having them do the project for Chapter 1 (TR Master 1-5, *The Marketing Mix in Action*).

You can also use some of the critical thinking and discussion questions from the *Teacher's Edition* and the *Teacher's Resources* to stimulate thinking and have students apply the concepts to their own lives. Often this type of activity works well in cooperative groups. Such a group usually encourages more participation. There are many activities labeled as cooperative activities, and many other activities can easily be turned into cooperative activities.

Help Students Consolidate Learning. Once students have had the opportunity to learn the material, you want to give them opportunities to "consolidate" their learning. Consolidation activities usually consist of individual activities that require students to write or present what they have learned. These activities are sometimes called "summative activities," in that they encourage students to summarize and review what they have learned. Activities appropriate for this stage include journal writing and activities from the *Activity Buffet—Content Review, Games,* and *Vocabulary*. Answering the "Review Concepts" and "Think Critically" in the student text "Chapter Review" section also helps students consolidate learning. When students finish these activities, they should be ready for an assessment on the objectives.

Vary the Activities

Certainly if you lecture every day and just have students read the text and answer questions, students will get bored. However, a certain amount of routine is necessary to provide order and calm in the classroom. We recommend having a consistent format, but varying the nature, content, and types of activities. The first and last five minutes of the day should have a consistent format and routine. See "Develop a Classroom Management Plan," pages 13–15.

Variety is especially important if you teach in an 80- or 90-minute block. Once you account for your five opening and closing minutes, you have 70 or 80 minutes to fill. Lecturing for that whole time will not benefit your students. Having students involved in a variety of activities would be more beneficial. The *Marketing Dynamics* program provides a wide variety of types and lengths of activities to use in block and regular scheduling. Consult the *Activity Buffet* in this handbook for generic activities that can be used with any topic.

The types of activities can include small group discussions, hands-on activities, individual writing and seat-work, individual reading of the text followed by small group discussions, working on computers and the Internet, group presentations, guest speakers, and field trips. Suggestions for all these types of activities appear in the *Student Workbook, Teacher's Edition,* and *Teacher's Resources.*

You might want to organize your class time into mini-sessions, varying in length from 10 to 30 minutes. Use a timer to demarcate mini-sessions and to help students stay on task. Especially useful is a timer that can be placed on an overhead so that the students, as well as you, can see how much time is left for an activity. Vary mini-sessions of individual work with group work and whole class work.

Students often complain that in block scheduling, teachers do not allow time for homework. Consequently, you might want to schedule some time into your lesson plan during which students can work on assignments for your class only.

Incorporate Assessment

Assessment is a key part of lesson planning and learning. See the separate section "Assessment."

How to Manage Activities in the Classroom

One of the things that will make your marketing classes successful and popular is the incorporation of activities. As mentioned previously, activities help students get more involved in their learning. Activities can also be fun and motivating. We especially urge you to do the Part Opener Activities, even those few that take some extra planning and preparation to gather the materials. You will reap benefits throughout the semester just from doing these activities.

However, you must carefully plan how to manage the activities for success. Just as with your daily routine, activities will go more smoothly if you prepare the materials ahead of time and have a system for distribution and a system for organizing the class into groups.

The Part Opener Activities are located in the *Teacher's Resources.* For each Part Opener Activity, there is a worksheet for the students and detailed guidelines for the teacher. The teacher's guidelines provide a list of the materials you need and how to prepare them. The guidelines also provide a procedure that will help you manage both the materials and the students. Discussion questions are provided. A time frame is also provided to give you an idea of how long the activity may take. However, the time frame is likely to vary, depending on the number of students and their natures. Use a timer and let students know how much time remains; this will help them stay on task.

The many other activities in the program are discussion-based or require only readily available materials such as paper and pencil or poster board and colored markers. Develop ways to quickly organize your class into small groups or pairs. Be sure to change the composition of the groups periodically, to give students the opportunity to interact with different classmates.

Setting Up Your Classroom

Establish a good relationship with your school custodial staff. Let them know when you will be doing things in your classroom that may affect their work or routine. Share with them why you are doing activities with the students and how these activities help prepare students for the business world. For example, if you rearrange the furniture for an activity, let the custodial staff know that they are to leave the furniture in the new arrangement. Also explain why; for example, say that you have rearranged the room so that students can do a simulation of international trading.

Let the custodial staff know how much you appreciate their help and how much they are helping you teach. Encourage your students to thank the custodial staff, too. Remind your students of the marketing concept and how everyone in an organization contributes to its success.

Debriefing

After each activity, especially the Part Opener Activities, you should debrief yourself, that is, you should evaluate how well the activity went and what you might do differently next time to improve the experience.

How will you know if the activity was successful? The following are some indicators:

- Students act like they are enjoying the activity by smiling and cooperating.
- When students ask, "When are you going to do this activity again?" or "When can we do another activity?"
- Students give good answers on their worksheets and during the discussion.
- When even one student thanks you.
- You might not find out whether this activity is successful until you continue teaching more concepts. Then you will realize that students are using their experiences from the activities to build their knowledge.

Here are some questions you can ask yourself to help develop ways to make the activities work even better:

- What worked?
- What did not work?
- What do you want to change for next time?
- Is there anything new you would like to try?
- How will I do this activity in the future?

Using the Internet as a Teaching Tool

The Internet is a fact of life for most businesses. Even businesses that do not have full-fledged sales Web sites at least have an informational site on the Web. Many businesses also use the Internet for purchasing and inventory maintenance.

The Internet is also a major resource for people searching for jobs and employers searching for workers. Major corporations have "Careers" and "Job Opportunities" links on their corporate Web sites. The federal government has online job notices and applications. Many Web sites provide guidelines and tips to help job seekers be successful in finding the right job. Many Web sites enable job seekers to post their resumes for interested employers to search.

No longer are newspapers and magazines only in paper form. They are on the Internet, along with many other content resources and databases that before the Internet were only obtainable with great difficulty. Students need to know how to access this information, both for career and personal success.

Because of the increasing presence and use of the Internet in the business world, educators need to teach students how to use the Internet effectively. Every chapter in the *Marketing Dynamics* student text has Internet activities in the Chapter Review, under the heading "Connect to the Internet." These activities specifically ask students to solve marketing problems by using the Internet. In addition, the "Explore Careers" section of the Chapter Review often asks students to visit Web sites for job and career information.

Many students find it more exciting to read materials online and use the Internet. You can use Internet activities to stimulate interest and excitement in marketing. If students do not have Internet access in your room, arrange for periodic class sessions in the computer lab where you can help students use the Internet effectively.

Think about establishing a blog (Web log— online journal) for your course. Many people think it is easier to set up than a Web site. You can use it to communicate with students and parents.

Be sure you teach students how to be safe on the Internet. Adhere to all of your school's guidelines on Internet usage.

Teaching the Learner with Special Needs

Most classrooms have students with a wide array of abilities and needs, from students who need a great deal of support and help to those who learn quickly and easily. Adapting daily lessons to the needs of all these students can be challenging. The table on the following pages provides descriptions of several types of special needs that students may have, along with teaching strategies that may be helpful in working with them.

Assessment

Assessment can and should include a wide array of activities, including tests and quizzes, written and oral reports, electronic and multimedia presentations, skits and role plays. Assessments should also be varied to accommodate the various learning styles of students. A student who does poorly on multiple-choice tests might do very well on a written report. Someone who is a visual learner might have more success preparing a poster than preparing an essay or a written report.

Various forms of assessment need to be used with students in order to evaluate the various

(Continued on page 35)

Adapting Lessons for Learners of Varying Abilities

	Learning Disabled*	Mentally Disabled*	Behaviorally or Emotionally Disabled*
Description	Students with learning disabilities (LD) have neurological disorders that interfere with their ability to store, process, or produce information, creating a "gap" between ability and performance. These students are generally of average or above-average intelligence. Examples of learning disabilities are distractibility, spatial problems, and reading comprehension problems.	Students with mental disabilities (MD) have subaverage general intellectual functioning that exists with deficits in adaptive behavior. These students are slower than others their age in using memory effectively, associating and classifying information, reasoning, and making judgments.	Students with behavioral or emotional disabilities exhibit undesirable behaviors or emotions, which may, over time, adversely affect educational performance. Their inability to learn cannot be explained by intellectual, social, or health factors. They may be inattentive, withdrawn, timid, restless, defiant, impatient, unhappy, fearful, unreflective; lack initiative; have negative feelings and actions; and blame others.
Teaching Strategies	• Help students get organized. • Give short oral directions. • Use drill exercises. • Give prompt cues during student performance. • Let students with poor writing skills use a computer. • Break assignments into small segments and assign only one segment at a time. • Demonstrate skills and have students model them. • Give prompt feedback. • Use continuous assessment to mark students' daily progress. • Prepare materials at varying levels of ability. • Shorten the number of items on exercises, tests, and quizzes. • Provide more hands-on activities.	• Use concrete examples to introduce concepts. • Make learning activities consistent. • Use repetition and drills spread over time. • Provide work folders for daily assignments. • Use behavior management techniques, such as behavior modification, in the area of adaptive behavior. • Encourage students to function independently. • Give students extra time to both ask and answer questions while giving hints to answers. • Avoid doing much walking around while talking to MD students as this is distracting for them. • Give simple directions and read them over with students. • Use objective test items and hands-on activities because students generally have poor writing skills and difficulty with sentence structure and spelling.	• Call students' names or ask them questions when you see their attention wandering. • Call on students randomly rather than in a predictable sequence. • Move around the room frequently. • Improve students' self-esteem by giving them tasks they can perform well, increasing the number of successful achievement experiences. • Decrease the length of time for each activity. • Use hands-on activities instead of using words and abstract symbols. • Decrease the size of the group so each student can actively participate. • Make verbal instructions clear, short, and to the point.

(Continued)

*We appreciate the assistance of Dr. Debra O. Parker, North Carolina Central University, with this section.

	Academically Gifted	**Limited English Proficiency**	**Physically Disabled**
Description	Students who are academically gifted are capable of high performance as a result of general intellectual ability, specific academic aptitude, and/or creative or productive thinking. Such students have vast resources of general knowledge and high levels of vocabulary, memory, and abstract reasoning.	Students with a limited proficiency in the English language generally speak English as their second language. Such students may be academically quite capable, but they lack the language skills needed to reason and comprehend abstract concepts.	Students who have physical disabilities include individuals who are orthopedically impaired, visually impaired, speech-impaired, deaf, hard-of-hearing, hearing-impaired, and health-impaired (cystic fibrosis, epilepsy). Strategies will depend on the specific disability.
Teaching Strategies	• Provide many opportunities for creative behavior. • Make assignments that call for original work, independent learning, critical thinking, problem solving, and experimentation. • Show appreciation for creative efforts. • Respect unusual questions, ideas, and solutions these students provide. • Encourage students to test their ideas. • Provide opportunities and give credit for self-initiated learning. • Avoid over-supervising these students. • Avoid relying too heavily on prescribed curricula. • Allow time for reflection. • Resist immediate and constant evaluation. This causes students to be afraid to use their creativity. • Avoid comparisons with other students, which applies subtle pressure to conform.	• Use a slow but natural rate of speech, speak clearly, use shorter sentences, and repeat concepts in several ways. • Act out questions using gestures with hands, arms, and the whole body. Use demonstrations and pantomime. Ask questions that can be answered by a physical movement such as pointing, nodding, or manipulating materials. • When possible, use pictures, photos, and charts. • Write key terms on the chalkboard. Point to the terms as you use them. • Corrections should be limited and appropriate. Do not correct grammar or usage errors in front of the class, which can cause embarrassment. • Give honest praise and positive feedback through your voice tones and visual articulation whenever possible. • Encourage students to use language to communicate, allowing them to use their native language to ask/answer questions when they are unable to do so in English. • Integrate students' cultural background into class discussions. • Use cooperative learning where students have opportunities to practice expressing ideas without risking language errors in front of the entire class.	• Seat visually and hearing-impaired students near the front of the classroom. Speak clearly and say out loud what you are writing on the chalkboard. • To reduce the risk of injury in lab settings, ask students about any conditions that could affect their ability to learn or perform. • Rearrange lab equipment or the classroom and make modifications as needed to accommodate any special need. • Investigate assistive technology devices that can improve students' functional capabilities. • Discuss specific solutions or modifications with the physically disabled student. He or she has experience with overcoming his or her disability and may have suggestions you may not have considered. • Let the student know when classroom modifications are being made and allow him or her to test them out before class. • Ask advice from a special education teacher, school nurse, or physical therapist. • Plan field trips that can include all students.

aspects of achievement. Written tests can be used to evaluate mastery of specific concepts and facts. Other methods, such as reports and presentations, are often better for evaluating achievement of the higher-order skills of application, analysis, synthesis, and evaluation.

Tests and Quizzes

Tests and quizzes can be used as a key part of the learning process. In the mastery learning approach, tests and quizzes are used to help students learn. In this approach, testing becomes a tool to help students learn, not a final judgment. The results of tests and quizzes are used to identify areas that need further work. These results are reviewed so that the student is aware of what he or she has learned and what he or she has yet to master. This information is used by the student and the teacher to help the student learn those topics not yet mastered. The student is given additional chances to take a test or quiz and show mastery.

Mastery learning also has the philosophy that you should tell students exactly what you want them to learn and remember. Rather than have them guessing, you provide a list of objectives and say, "This is the content that will be on the next test." Students can then spend their energy on learning the important concepts and facts that you want them to know. In this situation, most students can learn and achieve mastery.

In the mastery learning system, tests and quizzes are not the only bases for determining a student's grade. Tests and quizzes are used to determine whether a student has mastered the basic concepts of the course. To earn Bs and As, students can be given opportunities to do projects on topics of their own choosing (with teacher approval), and for these they can show achievement through written reports, electronic presentations, posters, and oral presentations.

A point grading system is often used to determine a student's final grade, based on test and quiz results and additional projects. See "Mastery Learning: A Point Grading System."

The *Marketing Dynamics* program provides chapter tests in the *Teacher's Resources*. On the **Exam**View® *Assessment Suite CD*, you will find the **Exam**View software that enables you to create a variety of tests and quizzes. There are 25 percent new questions in the **Exam**View testbank for each chapter. You can also add your own questions.

National Standards and Assessment

The National Standards can be used to provide the objectives for planning your curriculum and your assessments. The performance indicators for the *Business Administration Core Standards* and *Marketing Core Standards* are correlated to each chapter. These performance indicators appear in the Lesson Planning Guides in the *Teacher's Edition* and in the *Teacher's Resources*.

Authentic Assessment

Authentic assessment shows of how a student applies learned concepts to a realistic situation. For each chapter in *Marketing Dynamics*, the *Teacher's Resources* "Chapter Teaching Strategies: Review and Assess" includes an authentic assessment activity.

Performance Assessment

Performance assessment is a type of assessment that allows the student to show mastery by "performing" one or more tasks related to one or more objectives. Often, authentic assessments and performance assessments are similar or even the same. For example, suppose the objective is "Identify three types of influences on business buying behavior." An authentic/performance assessment would give the student a business buying-scenario, and ask the student to identify the three influences on that business buyer.

In addition, many of the activities and projects described in the *Teacher's Edition* annotations and the *Teacher's Resources* can be used for performance and authentic assessment.

Portfolios

Another type of performance assessment that is frequently used by teachers today is the portfolio. A *portfolio* consists of a selection of students' work that represents their performance over a period of time, such as a semester. Portfolios represent the students' finest works and provide examples of their accomplishments. Part of the challenge to students is to select their best works to showcase their achievements. Items can be chosen to provide evidence of employability skills as well as academic skills. Students might include the following items in their portfolios:

- classwork samples that show mastery of specific skills, such as photographs, video recordings, tests, and other written assessments

- writing samples that show communication skills
- a resume
- letters of recommendation that document specific career-related skills
- certificates of completion
- awards and recognition

A portfolio can be assembled at the culmination of a course, to provide evidence of learning. The student writes a self-assessment that explains what has been accomplished, what has been learned, what strengths the student has gained, and any areas that need improvement. This self-assessment usually appears at the beginning of the portfolio. Guidelines for students on how to assemble a portfolio, along with a rubric, can be found in the *Activity Buffet—Assessment: Portfolio.*

Portfolios may be presented to the class by the students. The items in the portfolio can also be discussed with the teacher in light of educational goals and outcomes. Portfolios should remain the property of students when they leave the course. Course portfolios can be used as a source of items for a career portfolio.

Chapter 50 of *Marketing Dynamics* discusses the use of a portfolio in a job interview situation. Students can take materials from their course portfolios to place into a job search portfolio. In the student text, Figure 50-14 (page 702) lists the types of items a student might place in a job search portfolio.

Self-Assessment

The ability to assess one's own knowledge, progress, and achievement will be critical to success in the future. Workers who can assess what they do well and what they need to learn, and then pursue what they need to learn, will have a much better chance of success than workers who cannot assess themselves in this way.

Educators do students a favor if they teach them how to evaluate themselves honestly and realistically. The mastery learning approach is one way to do this. When students get their tests back, they can see how well they have done and what they need to do to reach the 80 percent or better level. If students have trouble doing this on their own, have a conference with them each time you return a test. Show them how to use the grade and the marked test to understand how well they did and what they need to learn to do better. Then work with them to set a goal and a way to achieve that goal. For example, if the student is having trouble

remembering the Four Ps, show the student how to use flashcards, self-testing, and mnemonic devices to help remember this type of information.

Also give students the opportunity to grade their own work before they turn it in to you. Self-assessment might work particularly well with the projects in the *Teacher's Resources*. Each project has a checklist for students to use to make sure they have included the required parts of the project. You might use the checklist as a basis or beginning for self-assessment.

You might also give students the opportunity to develop their own assessment criteria/rubrics. For example, you can ask the class, "How should I evaluate you on teamwork? Give me a list of criteria." Have teams of students develop lists, share their lists, then decide on the key criteria. Then have the class suggest a range of points for each criterion. You might show them how to use a rubric first, for example, the "Participation Evaluation: Individual" in the *Activity Buffet—Communication.* Explain how to use this form, and give them the opportunity to use it to evaluate themselves and their group mates. Once they have mastered using this form, then have them develop one for evaluating teamwork.

Using Rubrics

The term *alternative assessment* is often used to refer to assessments that cannot be easily graded right and wrong, the way an objective test can be graded. Alternative assessments usually include authentic assessment, performance assessment, and portfolios. To evaluate student progress and accomplishments when alternative assessment is used, a different form of assessing mastery or achievement is required. One method teachers have successfully used is a rubric.

A *rubric* consists of a set of criteria that includes specific descriptors or standards that can be used to arrive at performance scores for students. A point value is given for each set of descriptors, leading to a range of possible points to be assigned, usually from 1 to 5. The criteria can also be weighted. The rubric is usually written as a form that can be filled out for each student. This method of assessment reduces the variability involved in grading performances, which leads to fair and consistent scoring. The criteria clearly indicate to students the various levels of mastery of a task. Students are even able to assess their own achievement based on the criteria.

When using rubrics, students should get a copy of the rubric/criteria at the beginning of the assignment. Then they can focus their efforts on what needs to be done to reach a certain level of performance or quality. They have a clear understanding of your expectations of achievement. These rubrics allow you to assess a student's performance and arrive at a performance score. Students can see what levels they have reached and what levels they can still strive to reach.

Though you may want to design your own rubrics, several generic rubric forms are included in the *Activity Buffet—Communication*. Examples include "Participation Evaluation: Individual" and "Participation Evaluation: Team."

Planning Assessments

Assessments must be planned along with your curriculum. Your assessment plan should include all items that will be used to determine a student's grade, including tests, quizzes, reports, projects, class participation, participation in role plays and skits, and work habits. You need to know how many tests and quizzes you will give. You should also determine how many assignments (reports, projects, etc.) you will give.

It is very beneficial to have the dates for tests and quizzes on your calendar. Dates when other assignments are due should also be on your calendar. See Figure H-1. Sometimes it is useful to have the same types of things due on the same days of the week. For example, tests and quizzes are scheduled for Fridays. Other kinds of assignments are due on Wednesdays.

You will also need to develop your grading system. Do you want to use percentages or points when you grade? Do you want to offer options for grades? Will all tests/quizzes be the same value? How much will each assignment be worth? How will you determine the grade for each assignment? You may want to develop your own rubrics for the various assignments. For one approach to grading, see the section, "Mastery Learning: A Point Grading System," page 24.

Using Rewards in the Classroom

Teachers vary on whether they like to use rewards in the classroom. If you do use a reward system, make it fair so that everyone has an opportunity to earn a reward. Have team rewards and individual rewards.

A popular reward for students is candy and other snack foods, but this type of reward is not always the best for students' health. There are many alternatives to food rewards. So use the food rewards sparingly.

You can prepare a set of "Marketing Mix Diamonds." Prepare copies of the diamond found in student text Figure 1-9 (page 25) or use Master 1-4 in the *Teacher's Resources*, page 42. Laminate them for long-lasting use. When a student gives a right answer or achieves something reward-worthy, give him or her a "diamond." When a student gathers a certain number of diamonds, he or she can turn them in for a bonus point in the point grading system. The diamonds can also be turned in for school-store coupons or other rewards. You can post a list of how many diamonds are needed for specific rewards.

Another reward that students like is certificates. You can use a word-processing program to quickly design a variety of certificates. Use certificates to reward and reinforce academic achievement as well as work habits and community service. For example, the student who raises the most money for a fund-raiser could get a salesperson certificate. The student who is most helpful to others could get an "MVP" most valuable person certificate. The student who achieves an academic goal, such as receiving all *As* on a report card, could get an academic achievement certificate. Students can also be awarded certificates for DECA participation. You can make your own DECA certificates or buy certificates from DECA Images on the DECA Web site.

Keeping Yourself Up-to-Date

With all the demands of teaching, you may wonder how you can keep up with the changes in marketing. The good news is that the basics of marketing do not change. The basics that you learned in school still remain. However, the examples, that is, what is actually going on in the real world, change almost daily.

The second bit of good news is that changes in marketing are all around you. Listen to the news on the radio while driving to work. Watch the nightly TV news. Skim the business section of your local newspaper. Sign up for some electronic newsletters. If you do any of these even occasionally, you will find numerous examples and ideas to use in your classroom.

Also, attend professional meetings and workshops. The annual Conclave sponsored by MBAResearch focuses specifically on marketing, entrepreneurship, and management (for information on all of MBAResearch's programs, visit www.mbaresearch.org). If your school supports a career and technical student organization, such as DECA, attend the conferences and competitions. These gatherings provide opportunities to network with other marketing teachers.

Building Academic Skills

Why should a career and technical teacher be interested in academic skills? Because all your students need to be proficient at the basic skills in order to succeed in work and in life. In addition, the proliferation high-stakes academic testing means that career and technical teachers are feeling some pressure to help students achieve in these tests.

Integrating Academics

The importance of academic achievement has been emphasized in recent years. The *No Child Left Behind Act of 2001* brought this to national attention. The act also instituted a program of accountability testing in the following key areas: English, reading, language arts, math, science, foreign languages, civics and government, economics, arts, history, and geography. Career and technical education teachers have been encouraged to incorporate academics into their programs to help students do well on these crucial tests.

Marketing is a natural for incorporating these subjects because marketing touches on many aspects of life and learning. The *Marketing Dynamics* program supports student growth and achievement in key academic areas in several ways. Some subjects are explicitly covered in the text (economics, government, language arts). Other subject areas are covered as background or supporting information to marketing concepts (reading, language arts, art, history, geography, foreign language). Analogies to concepts from science and social studies are used as appropriate. One subject, math, is used as a tool to understand various marketing concepts. Another subject, language arts (writing and communication) is presented as a key skill for marketing and career success.

For suggestions on improving reading and writing, see "Helping Students Become Better Readers and Writers," following. For details on how the *Marketing Dynamics* program incorporates academics, see the *Teacher's Edition: Introduction for Teachers*, "Integrating Academics," section.

Helping Students Become Better Readers and Writers

One of the major goals of high school is to develop a literate citizenry. Even though you are a marketing teacher, you need to be concerned about the ability of your students to read and write. Many marketing professions require members to be excellent readers and writers. Reading and writing skills help students be more successful, no matter what career they pursue. Marketing, as a high school subject, offers a multitude of opportunities to help students develop their reading and writing skills.

The first thing to do is to get students excited about their textbook and the subject of marketing. Goodheart-Willcox hopes that the race car on the cover will peak their interest. Use the reproducible, "Why a Race Car," in the *Activity Buffet—Reading* to start a discussion about the textbook and marketing. To get students familiar with their textbook, have them do the "What's in My Textbook" activity in the *Activity Buffet—Reading*.

The *Marketing Dynamics* student text was specifically developed to engage students' interest and entice them to read the text, while at the same time presenting marketing concepts in a clear way. For a detailed discussion of how *Marketing Dynamics* was developed specifically to promote reading and understanding, please see the *Teacher's Edition: A Fresh Approach to Marketing Education*," pages T24–T28.

SQ3R and KWL

Reading specialists have determined that students' understanding and recall of what they read improves when they are actively engaged before reading (*prereading*), during reading, and after reading. One way to engage students in this way is called *SQ3R*. It stands for *s*urvey, *q*uestion, *r*ead, *r*ecite, *r*eview. Guidelines for this strategy are in the *Activity Buffet—Reading*, "SQ3R Student Instructions" and "SQ3R Worksheet." Another strategy is called KWL, which stands for "Know, Want to Know, and Learned." Guidelines for this strategy are in the *Activity Buffet—Reading*, "KWL: Teacher Guidelines."

Prereading

The purpose of prereading activities is to acquaint students with the general topic of the piece to be read. Prereading includes activities designed to activate prior knowledge, that is, help bring to awareness what students already know about the topic of the piece.

Prereading activities create or bring to awareness background knowledge that will help students understand what they read. Prereading activities include scanning the piece to be read and predicting what you will learn from reading the piece.

The *Marketing Dynamics* program includes many prereading activities. A key prereading activity is the Part Opener Activity, which gets students actively engaged in an activity that causes them to think about the topic of the part and to realize that they *do* know something about the topic. In addition, each chapter in the *Teacher's Edition* and the *Teacher's Resources* opens with an introductory activity designed to preview the content of the chapter. The *Teacher's Edition* also has a variety of "Prereading" and "Vocabulary Builder" activities for each chapter. The *Activity Buffet—Reading* lists generic prereading activities.

During Reading

The goal during reading activities is to help students understand the text and remember key concepts. Many students need to be taught to make their minds active *while* they read. Many students just "run their eyes" over the text and think that they are reading. It is not just a matter of reminding students to focus on the text. Good readers are engaged with the text while they read. In their minds, several processes are going on, in addition to decoding the text: They are seeing pictures of what they are reading, like a video. They are commenting on the text, e.g., *That's interesting,* or *I disagree.* They are connecting the text to their experiences, e.g., *I remember when I did something like that.* They are using the text to answer a question that they have, e.g., *So that's why marketing research is not always right.* They are questioning the text, e.g., *Why does the author think that?* They are responding emotionally to the text, e.g., by laughing or crying. They also are monitoring their own understanding, e.g., *I don't understand what I just read.*

You do not need to be a reading expert to help students become more-active readers (although you may want to read some books on helping students improve their reading comprehension and implement some of their strategies). The *Marketing Dynamics* student text is structured to help students engage in more-active reading. To help students visualize what they are reading, the text uses vivid, concrete descriptions that students can easily picture. If they still have trouble picturing the words, many descriptions have a photo reference. This photo provides a visual image of what was just described in the text.

Another feature of the text helps students learn to question while they read: questions included in the text itself. The question in the text follows naturally from the previous sentence. The text following the question answers it. For example, on student text page 55, the following appears: "The business customer uses the products it buys for the business. How are products used in a business? There are three types of business uses . . ."

The "Reality Check" feature also helps students learn to question, review, and apply what they have just read. This brief feature, placed after a section of text, asks students to apply what they have just read to something in their lives or to common experiences.

In addition, many of the activities in the *Student Workbook, Teacher's Edition,* and the *Teacher's Resources* can be used as during reading activities.

You can also help students learn to read more effectively by occasionally having them read out loud or to themselves a short portion of text, then discussing it with them in detail. Ask students to summarize what they just read, describe what they visualized, explain whether they agree, share what the section reminded them of, ask any questions they still have, tell you anything that they did not understand. You can use the bookmarks provided on the master, "Questions to Ask While Reading," in the *Activity Buffet—Reading* to help you with this activity. This might be a good activity to do first in small groups, then have each group report to the class. After the discussion, have students write a reaction paper. They can use the "Reaction Paper" form in the *Activity Buffet—Communication.*

Another way to help students improve their reading is to teach them how to recognize when they have *not* understood what they are reading, and what to do to help them understand difficult text. Use the master, "What to Do When You Don't Understand," in the *Activity Buffet—Reading.* This master explains how to tell when you do not understand what you are reading, and what steps to take to figure out what the text means.

After Reading

What readers do after reading often determines how well they remember what they read. Two of the three *R*s in SQ3R speak to this: recite and review. Writing could also be added to this list. In short, readers must in some way go over what they have read to firm-up the information in their minds. In constructivist theory, this is called *consolidation,* that is, organizing the information in a way that you can easily retrieve it again from memory.

The SQ3R and KWL reading strategies, presented in the *Activity Buffet—Reading* teach students ways to interact with the text they read and consolidate their knowledge. These two strategies combine prereading, during reading, and after reading activities into a coherent, easy-to-apply strategy. Use the masters in the *Activity Buffet— Reading* to help you teach these strategies to your students.

An important way for students to consolidate their knowledge is to have them organize the chapter content in a format that makes sense to them and helps them remember the content. For some students, a traditional outline works. Others will find a graphic organizer more helpful. Encourage students to organize their notes in a way that works for them.

In addition, the *Marketing Dynamics* program provides many ways to help students review, consolidate, and use what they have read in the text. Each student text chapter has a *Chapter Review*. This section provides a bulleted list of key points under the heading "Remember This." Students can use this as a quick review of the key points in the chapter that they just read. The "Review Concepts" section provides questions to review chapter content. The "Think Critically" section provides questions that require students to use the chapter content and their higher order thinking skills.

Because waiting until the end of the chapter to review content is often not effective, the *Teacher's Edition* provides an annotation to help you provide review and critical thinking questions throughout the chapter. The annotation "Review It Now" is placed on the page where a section of content ends. The annotation then specifies which terms to review and which questions under "Review Concepts" and "Think Critically" to answer to review the preceding text.

The *Chapter Review* sections "Connect to Business," "Explore Careers," and "Connect to the Internet" require students to apply concepts learned in the chapter to new situations. Many of the activities in the *Student Workbook, Teacher's Edition,* and the *Teacher's Resources* can be used as after-reading activities. In addition, the following

Activity Buffet categories provide generic activities designed to reinforce newly read content: *Content Review, Games,* and *Vocabulary.*

Beyond the Textbook

There are many fun and easy-to-read books on marketing, from *Marketing for Dummies* to *The 22 Immutable Laws of Marketing.* New books appear in bookstores frequently. Get your school library to designate funds to buy some new, popular marketing books each year. Assign book reports, but create excitement about the books first. When a new marketing book is published, try to acquire a copy, bring it in, and talk it up to students. Give extra credit to students who find newly (or at least fairly recently) published marketing books and bring them to the attention of the class. (If they cannot buy the book, they can bring in a review or borrow a copy from the library.) To get credit, they must explain why this book is worth reading. In your point grading system, you can award extra points for each book report submitted. You might even have a contest for the student who reads the most marketing books, with an appropriate award. Students can use the "Book Report" form in the *Activity Buffet—Communication.*

Encourage students to also read short pieces that appear in newspapers, magazines, and on the Internet. Such articles are an excellent way to keep up-to-date on the most current changes, advances, and news. Students can use the "Article Report" or "Reaction Paper" forms in the *Activity Buffet—Communication.*

Writing

Writing well is a highly prized ability in the business world. Many marketing careers require excellent writing skills, for example, advertising, marketing communications, public relations, and marketing research. Even many sales jobs, especially B2B, require the sales representatives to write reports and proposals for clients. As a marketing teacher, you can help your students polish their writing skills. Many of the activities and projects in the *Marketing Dynamics* program require students to write a report or other document, so you will have many opportunities to help students improve their writing.

A great way to learn about your students' writing abilities is to assign them to write their autobiographies. It is also a great way for you to learn about your students early in the term. If this is their first writing assignment, describe what you expect in a written assignment. See "The First Day: First Assignment," page 16.

You might also (early in the semester) want to go over the "General Sender Skills" in student text Chapter 49, "Communicating for Success," page 674. You might also explain your system for submitting revisions as well as your system for students to act as peer reviewers on their writing. These systems will be especially important if you require that all written work be submitted error-free. Teach students how to review their own work and the work of peers.

Training students to turn in error-free written work is extremely valuable. If written work is handed in with errors, circle the errors and ask students to make corrections and resubmit the work error-free. At first, students will be upset with having to redo an assignment. However, emphasize the fact that the business world expects written work to be error-free.

If you have time, you might have students research situations in which errors in written communications created large and expensive mistakes. For example, in August 2006, the person responsible for new maps on the Chicago transit system did not check the maps before they were printed. The result? Three major typos in the new maps created confusion for transit riders. One of the typos was the wrong telephone number to call for transit information! The worker had transposed two of the numbers. (Transposition is a common typo.) The Chicago Transit Authority had to correct, reprint, and repost all of the maps, at a cost of $75,000. The worker was fired.

Students must learn that reviewing their work for errors involves more than just running the spelling and grammar checker in their word-processing program. They should reread their final work through slowly, twice. Once to pay attention to the sense and logic of the work, and the second time to look for grammatical and spelling errors that a word-processing program will not catch.

Connecting to the Work World

One of the things that teenagers crave is to know where they might fit into the adult world. When teens see a future for themselves, they are more likely to stay in school and to do their best. One of the benefits of career education is that it helps students see a future for themselves. As marketing teachers, we can help our students by connecting them to the world of work.

Giving students opportunities to experience the world of work can be one of the most fun and exciting aspects of career education. Some of your programs may have a cooperative education work component, which is one of the best ways to give students a real taste of the work world. Your schools may also have established programs for job shadowing and career days. Whether or not your school has such programs, the *Marketing Dynamics* program provides many activities and suggestions for showing your students the work world.

The *Marketing Dynamics* student text itself exposes students to many aspects of the work world. In addition, in the student text in each "Chapter Review," the section "Connect to Business" specifically suggests ways to connect the chapter content to some aspect of the business world. Students can use their workplace, if they are working, or visit local stores to find answers to the questions and projects posed in this section. The "Explore Careers" section also introduces students to the work world by showing them how to find information on a wide variety of careers.

The *Teacher's Edition* and the *Teacher's Resources* have annotations/teaching strategies called "Workplace Connection." These activities were designed specifically for students who are currently working. However, students who are not working can visit local stores or other businesses, or use businesses on the Internet for the activities.

In addition, the *Teacher's Resources* has a section "Speakers and Field Trips" for each chapter. This section provides a wide variety of ways to take your students to the business world or bring the business world to your students. This section also includes suggestions of people to interview. You should always do some groundwork before sending students out to do interviews, so that the same person is not inundated with requests to do interviews with students. When there is only one person available with the requisite qualification and experience, invite that person to class for a TV-style interview. Have all students prepare questions, as if each one were going to do the interview. You can either then designate one person to be the interviewer, or have several students take turns. You can also have the audience (the rest of the class) participate during a question-and-answer period.

The Advisory Board

As you seek ways to involve students with the world of work, consider establishing an advisory board for your marketing program. An advisory board can be an invaluable resource for ideas on how to connect your students to the work world and for contacts to make those connections happen.

Invite local business people to be on your board. Consider including people from local colleges and nonprofit organizations. If necessary, consult with your local chamber of commerce for names of possible participants. Often, the large chains encourage employees to be involved with local schools. You might also consult the list of businesses that are partners with the career and technical student organization that your school sponsors. For example, DECA has a list of business partners who are part of the DECA National Advisory Board (see DECA's Web site: http://deca.org/nab_index.html). Because of their participation in and support of DECA, these companies might be interested in providing members to serve on your advisory board.

Incorporating Career and Technical Student Organizations

Career and technical student organizations (CTSOs) are another great way to get students involved in activities that prepare them for, and expose them to, the world of work. Participation in CTSOs gives students the opportunity to develop leadership skills, practice and apply marketing concepts, get involved in community service, and interact with business professionals. The *Marketing Dynamics* program refers specifically to DECA—An Association of Marketing Students, because that organization focuses on marketing, management, and entrepreneurship. However, the suggestions for DECA can often be applied to the other CTSOs.

One advantage of offering DECA or other CTSO is the exposure to business leaders that students receive. Whether your students compete, work on a project that requires contacting local businesses, or participate in a community service project, they are being exposed to the business environment as well as social situations. These experiences are invaluable to help students develop skills and attitudes that they need to be successful throughout their lives.

For more information on how the *Marketing Dynamics* program incorporates career and technical student organizations, see the *Teacher's Edition: Introduction for Teachers*, "Incorporating Career and Technical Student Organizations," section.

The School Store

One of the best teaching tools and ways to connect your students to the world of business is to have a real business operating in your classroom or school. A school-based enterprise (SBE) is like a piece of the real world, right in your school. Everything that happens in a "real" store happens in a school-based enterprise. Students often learn on their own, just by working in the school-based business. If a problem occurs in the store, you can use it as a "teachable moment" and help students learn concepts, ethics, and habits from the situation. A school-based enterprise also provides the opportunity for students to develop teamwork, communication, and leadership skills.

Those students who have operated a school-based enterprise are years ahead of those students who have not had the same opportunity. If you also teach an internship program, students with school store experience will be very easy to place in local businesses. You know their strengths and their abilities to solve problems and to work in a team environment. You have actually caught them doing a "great job" in a business environment and so can easily recommend them for various internship opportunities.

The opportunity to work in the school store will also be a great recruiting tool for your marketing program. As you know, marketing teachers must often recruit enough students to merit continuation of their programs. Having a school store is often a significant plus when describing the program to potential students.

Store Size

A school-based enterprise can be as simple or as complex, as large or as small, as your resources permit. Some schools operate a simple kiosk or pushcart that is open only during the morning hours when students arrive at school. Other schools have an actual retail space in the school, where they sell a large variety of snack, school, and clothing items.

Also keep in mind that students do not need a full-year, five-day-a-week, full-school-day enterprise to have a learning experience. Thus, school-based enterprises can take a variety of forms, including a store that is just open for the winter holiday business, a snack-and-school supplies store that is just open before school, or an e-commerce business. The main point is that students gain experience buying, pricing, monitoring inventory, promoting, selling, accounting, and solving problems.

The *Marketing Dynamics* student text has photographs taken from a school store. Examples of those photographs include student text Figures 28-6 (page 353), 28-11 (page 357), and 40-7 (page 537).

Focus on Curriculum

We recommend that the focus of the store be teaching the students, rather than making a profit (although making a profit is good and we realize that some schools/school programs rely on the income from their school-based enterprises). Students can gain experience as clerks in a variety of businesses. Only in a school store can they experience being in charge and responsible. We recommend that you set up and structure your school-based enterprise so that the students are in charge, with sufficient supervision so that they do not get themselves or the school in trouble.

A suggestion for you, the instructor, is to teach the curriculum first, then establish the store. Ask yourself, "What is running my class, the store or my curriculum?" If you want to offer a quality program, then your goal should be to teach the curriculum first with the store being the secondary focus.

If your goal is to make the school store a truly learning environment with the students assuming the ownership of the business, then you will need time to teach the curriculum to the students before you open the store. Schedule the grand opening for your store in November, and teach the concepts/performance indicators necessary for the store during the first months of school.

How to Start

There are as many ways to start a store as there are high school marketing instructors. Consequently, there is no one right or wrong way. Most teachers who operate a school store would suggest that you, as the teacher, oversee all the daily transactions and that you have adequate time allowed to do that.

Your store will become a focal point for the school; and if something goes wrong, you will definitely find out about it. It is important for the students to be aware of this scrutiny from the onset. You can use this as a motivator to keep your students doing their best and working hard.

The following is a checklist of steps to take before opening the store. Note: the students should perform most tasks listed below, with appropriate supervision. You will need to decide what issues should be decided by vote or contest, such as the name of the store. You also need to make sure that any school or municipal rules and laws are followed.

1. Decide when the store could be open and where it will be located. (place)
2. Prepare and administer a survey to determine what types of products the target market would purchase. (product, market, and marketing information)
3. Tabulate the survey findings, interpret them, and report to the class. (marketing information, analysis, and communication)
4. Decide the product mix for the store. (product)
5. Decide on a name for the store. (product, branding, promotion)
6. Establish a timeframe for opening of the store. (place)
7. Identify the tasks that must be accomplished to operate the store. (operations, management)
8. Meet with vendors/suppliers. (product, price, purchasing)
9. Decide on and make purchases. (product, purchasing)
10. Begin promotion activities. (promotion)
11. Arrange stock and decorate the store. (stocking, visual merchandising)
12. Provide training to students who will be operating cash registers, receiving inventory, performing accounting functions. (operations, sales, distribution, inventory)
13. Send out invitations to VIPs whom you would like to have at your grand opening. Ask for RSVPs so you can plan for enough refreshments. (promotion)
14. Plan a grand opening, including program and refreshments. (operations)
15. Have a grand opening ceremony with a ribbon cutting by all those involved. (promotion)

16. Open the store. (promotion, selling, operations, marketing information)

Preparing Students for Work in the Twenty-First Century

A key recommendation is to expose students to the workplace. For suggestions on how to do this, see "Connecting to the Work World," pages 41–44.

Attitude and Work Ethic

What do employers expect of employees? The following list (which you can also find as a reproducible in the *Activity Buffet—Workplace/Job Search Skills*) states the key behaviors expected by most employers:

Come to work everyday on time. Follow directions. Apply good listening skills. Concentrate on your work. Recognize problems and find solutions. Manage time effectively. Maintain a safe work environment. Be honest and dependable. Dress properly and practice good grooming. Be cooperative. Have a positive attitude. (Source: Poster, *What Do Employers Expect of Me as an Employee?* CWI Workforce Investment Board Youth Council, developed as result of a Department of Workforce Development Grant.)

You might have students do a cooperative activity in which small groups put together their own lists of what they think employers expect. Have groups share their lists. Then give them a copy of the above list, and have students compare them and discuss the similarities and differences. Students could also use the above list to generate role plays or skits that illustrate each behavior, and/or the result of the lack of each behavior.

A good way to show students that this list is not just made up is to invite a panel of business people to discuss attitude and work habits. Invite people from a variety of businesses and industries. Have students generate a list of questions. Send the guests the list of questions and the list of key behaviors. You should moderate the panel to make sure that key topics are addressed. If possible, arrange for the event to be audio or video recorded, so that students can listen to it again.

Students might be inclined to pay attention to what the panelists have to say when they realize that these are the people who have the power to hire and fire. One of the best comments (and one that has probably been said by many) from a community banker was, "I hire on attitude and I fire on attitude."

Multicultural and Global Awareness

The workplace of the twenty-first century is more diverse than any before it. There is diversity in both colleagues and customers. In addition, with foreign corporations establishing units in the United States, and U.S. companies branching out to foreign countries, workers are much more likely than before to work with foreigners.

The *Marketing Dynamics* student text tackles the issue of market diversity in Chapter 14, "A Diverse Marketplace." Demographic changes, ethnic groups, and cultural differences, as well as the dangers of stereotyping, are presented. Global awareness is increased in the two chapters on international trade, Chapters 12 and 13. Throughout the text, multicultural and global issues are presented as appropriate. For example, in Chapter 35, "Verbal and Nonverbal Communication," the potential problems of translation of brand names and advertising are addressed.

In addition, the *Teacher's Edition* introduces the "International Business Project," in Chapter 1. This project is carried throughout the text by the "International Business Project" annotations. Students set up an International Business Project Notebook, and record their responses to the International Business Project annotations that their teacher assigns.

For additional suggestions on how to help students value diversity, see "Strategies for Effective Teaching: Helping Students Value Diversity," pages 20–21.

Ethics

The perceived lack of ethics in the business world has been front-page news for years. The name Enron has become synonymous with "unethical business practices." We need to provide our students with some way to think about ethics and apply them to business situations. We do *not* want to interfere with students' individual ethics and beliefs. However, we *do* want to educate them about the qualities that most employers expect in their workers: honesty, integrity, responsibility, and confidentiality. We also want to encourage students to develop these qualities in themselves.

The *Marketing Dynamics* program tackles this issue in student text Chapter 5, "Social Responsibility." This chapter discusses the three aspects of business social responsibility: (1) be legal, (2) be ethical, and (3) be philanthropic. The chapter presents a model for ethical decision making, presented as Figure 5-7 (page 73). This model is also available as a transparency/reproducible master in the *Teacher's Resources*, Master 5-1, "Steps in Ethical Decision Making" (page 85). There are also activities in the *Activity Buffet—Decision Making and Ethics.*

If you prefer, you might want to use a simpler three-step ethical process, described by Kenneth H. Blanchard and Norman Vincent Peale in their book, *The Power of Ethical Management.* This book suggests three questions to ask about a decision to determine whether it is ethical:

- Is it legal?
- Is it balanced?
- How would I feel if my name were on the front page of the newspaper for everyone to see?

Team and Human Relations Skills

Employers often state that two of the reasons that employees are fired are because they cannot get along with others and they cannot work together as a team. The *Marketing Dynamics* program offers many opportunities to teach students how to work in a team and to help them develop good human relations skills (including communication). See "Strategies for Effective Teaching: Turning Your Class into a Team," pages 22–23.

In addition, the topics of interpersonal skills and teamwork in the workplace are presented in student text Chapter 51, "Achieving Success." To expand on this information, the *Activity Buffet—Parliamentary Procedure* provides additional information in the form of reproducibles that you can copy and give to students. Students can implement these concepts at meetings of student organizations, such as student government and DECA chapter meetings.

If you are the advisor of your DECA chapter, you can help reinforce the concepts of teamwork and interpersonal skills at DECA chapter meetings. Make sure that your DECA officers and chairpersons know how to conduct a meeting using parliamentary procedure. Before the first DECA chapter meeting, review the guidelines for meetings and parliamentary procedure with the entire class (or all the classes that will participate).

After the DECA meeting, have a debriefing with your DECA officers and chairpersons. First, compliment them on what went well. Then discuss what each individual could do to make the meetings run even better.

If possible, arrange a class trip to see how professionals conduct meetings. The local government might be one possibility. Another possibility might be to watch such a meeting on TV. Have students write a field trip or reaction report. You can have them use the "Field Trip Report" or "Reaction Paper" forms from the *Activity Buffet—Communication.*

Keeping Yourself Energized

Teaching is a challenging profession, both psychologically and physically. You will feel better and accomplish more if you find ways to keep yourself physically healthy and emotionally energized.

Each person has to develop his or her own ways of coping with the stresses of life, but you might want to take some cues from the advice we offer students in *Marketing Dynamics* student text, Chapter 51, "Achieving Success," the section on "Self-Management Skills," pages 718–724. The suggestions for health and organization are particularly relevant.

Teachers are particularly susceptible to communicable illnesses because students bring them in from all over. For this reason, it is particularly important to get enough rest, eat healthful foods, and exercise. As you probably know, lack of sleep not only makes you vulnerable to illnesses, but can also make you short-tempered with the students and have a negative outlook on life. Recent research indicates that lack of sleep may also lead to overeating and thus to obesity. During the school year, it might be advantageous to keep the same sleep-wake schedule, even on weekends. (This is good advice for your students, too!)

You may need to be more organized than ever before. You need to be organized so that you can get enough sleep every night, schedule in some exercise, get all your papers graded, and make time for your personal life. Exercise and time for yourself and your family are key components in managing stress and helping you live a balanced life.

As you may know, the bad days at school can be very bad. Develop ways to help yourself deal with the frustrations and the problems that arise. Look at your mission statement and remind yourself why you are a teacher.

Here are some more suggestions for ways to deal with the bad days of teaching:

- Write your mission statement if you have not already done so.
- Remind yourself of your reason for teaching.
- Collect inspirational books and read them.
- Find inspirational quotations and post them around your room and your home office.
- Review all the positive aspects of the day/week/month/year.
- Think about a student whom you helped or on whom you had a positive impact.
- Get away for a few minutes by using deep breathing or visualization.
- Get away for a few hours to rest or exercise.
- Be sure to take vacations and really get away.
- Watch the "Fish Philosophy" video (see "Resources" section).
- Read a book on positive attitude.
- Join your professional organization and get involved.
- Attend professional workshops.
- Read professional trade magazines and keep up-to-date on technology.
- Talk with a veteran teacher who has a positive attitude.
- Network with other marketing teachers.

The book by Dr. Seuss, *Oh, The Places You'll Go!* can provide inspiration for both teachers and students. The following lines may be particularly appropriate:

"You'll get mixed up, of course,
as you already know.
You'll get mixed up
with many strange birds as you go.
So be sure when you step,
step with care and great tact
and remember that Life's
a Great Balancing Act. . . .
And will you succeed?
Yes! You will, indeed!
(98 and ¾ percent guaranteed.)"

As teachers, we often get mixed up or confused. We will see strange students, strange parents, strange teachers. When we teach, we need to use tact. We also need to remember that we have to balance our school lives with our personal lives. It is a challenge to balance everything we need to do. However, we will succeed most of the time; and we will have a positive impact on our students, our schools, and our communities.

Activity Buffet

A dinner buffet is an offering of a variety of foods from which the diner can choose. An *Activity Buffet* is an offering of a variety of activities from which the teacher or student can choose. The activities in the Activity Buffet can be used with any chapter. In other words, they are not content-specific. For example, making flashcards and using them to review word definitions is an activity that can be used with any and all chapters.

The *Activity Buffet* is organized by type of activity. There are 12 categories currently on the *Activity Buffet—Assessment, Communication, Content Review, Decision Making and Ethics, Games, Getting To Know You, Parliamentary Procedure, Reading, Role Plays, Vocabulary, Warm-Ups,* and *Workplace/Job Search Skills.* For example, the flashcard activity is a vocabulary activity; therefore, directions for flashcards appear in the *Vocabulary* category.

How would you use the *Activity Buffet?* Suppose you have started Chapter 3. You want the students to do a vocabulary activity in class. Look over the choices in the *Vocabulary* category. You can use these activities in one of three ways. (1) You can select one of the activities and have all students do it as an individual activity. (2) You can select one of the activities and have students do it as a class or group activity. (3) You can give the students the option to choose any one of the activities. Reproduce a page of the *Vocabulary* activities, and distribute it to students, and let them choose which vocabulary activity they would like to do.

The activities are set up on pages so that they can be reproduced. Some of the pages just list the activity ideas. Other pages are actual worksheets or forms that can be reproduced for student or teacher use.

Students should have paper and pen/pencil available to use with these activities. Some activities may require additional simple materials, such as a stack of index cards.

Activity Buffet Categories

Assessment: Alternative

Main Concept. Write a summary or tell your marketing teacher the following: What is the main concept of this chapter? Why do you think this concept is important? Where might you see examples of this concept in your daily life or on the job? How might this concept affect you, either in your life now or in the future?

Poster. Create a poster that presents the main concepts in the chapter. Find photos or draw diagrams to illustrate the concepts. Use the words in the marketing terms list.

Short Story. Write a short story. The story should have characters and a plot. Build the story around the concepts in the chapter. Use the words in the marketing terms list.

Poem, Rap, or Song. Write a poem, rap, or song. The subject is the concepts in this chapter. Use the words in the marketing terms list. Perform your poem, rap, or song for the class.

Dialog. Imagine that two characters in the work world are discussing the concepts in this chapter. Give each of your characters a name. Then write a dialog for them. In this dialog, the characters discuss the concepts in this chapter. Use the words in the marketing terms list. Perform the dialog with a partner.

Skit. Write a skit based on the concepts in this chapter. Use the words in the marketing terms list. Perform the skit for the class.

Nursery Rhyme. Find a nursery rhyme or other short, published work; and change the story to include information and terms from the chapter. Include a copy of the original work with title, author, and source.

Assessment: Portfolio
Guidelines for Students

A *portfolio* is a collection of items that show your accomplishments. There are several types of portfolios. You may be asked to do one or all of the following types: course portfolio, employment portfolio, and career portfolio.

A *course portfolio* shows your accomplishments and growth in the concepts and content of a course, such as Marketing Foundations. A course portfolio shows that you have met the objectives of the course for the current grading period. This type of portfolio usually includes one or more sections in which you analyze your work and assess your own progress.

An *employment portfolio* shows your accomplishments and growth in a cooperative program, in other words, a career and technical education program that includes a work component. This portfolio will include all the items that you develop to help you in your employment and career search.

A *career portfolio* is a collection of documents that show your qualifications for a certain job or career. A career portfolio should be designed to impress a potential employer with your work skills and experience. A career portfolio is usually created just before you start a job search.

Your portfolio is separate and different from your class notebook. The class notebook is for *all* papers related to this class. The portfolio is a *selection* of your best documents to showcase your skills, abilities, and accomplishments.

1. Collect Documents and Other Items

Use your class notebook to save all written documents and electronic copies of your work. Electronic documents can be kept on a CD or DVD in a notebook or divider pocket. Also document through photographs any projects that do not fit in a notebook, such as a diorama.

2. Select

Review the portfolio checklist (provided on a separate sheet) for your portfolio. When the time comes to assemble your portfolio, go through the items collected in your notebook. Select the best examples for each section of the portfolio. You may not have documents for some sections until the end of the semester or the end of the year, for example, transcripts and awards.

3. Reflect

One of the values in preparing a portfolio is to think about each item you select. Think about why you selected that item. Think about what you learned while doing that activity. Think about what this item shows about your progress and accomplishments or your qualifications for a certain job or career. When your teacher requests that you write a reflection about one of the items, answer the following questions:

- Why did I choose this item?
- What growth does it show?
- What marketing concepts does it illustrate?
- What do I still need to work on?
- What would impress a potential employer?

Activity Buffet: Assessment

Assessment: Portfolio
Course Portfolio Contents Checklist

Use this checklist as a guide when selecting the items that should be in your course portfolio. You can also use it as the basis of your table of contents.

	Cover
	Include key information (name, class, date); you may enhance it with graphics
	Title Page
	Table of Contents
	Overview of Accomplishments
	What were your goals for this grading period? Did you accomplish them? What do you need to work on? What are your goals for the next grading period?
	Best Test
	Reflection on My Best Test
	Why do you think this was your best test? What does it show about your understanding of marketing concepts? What does it show about your style of learning or studying? What do you need to improve?
	Best Written Assignment
	Reflection on My Best Written Assignment
	Why did you choose this as your best written assignment? How did you feel while you were working on it? What does this piece show about your writing abilities? What does this piece show about your understanding of marketing concepts? What do you need to work on?
	Best Project
	Reflection on My Best Project
	Why did you choose this as your best project? How did you feel while you were working on it? What does this piece show about your understanding of marketing concepts? What do you need to work on?
	Hardest Assignment
	Reflection on My Hardest Assignment
	Why was this your hardest assignment? What processes did you use to help you finish this assignment? What did you learn from this assignment? How does the final result compare with your other work for this course?
	Worst Work
	Reflection on My Worst Work
	Why was this your worst work? What interfered with your doing better on this assignment? What could you do in the future on this kind of assignment so that you would produce better work?
	Self-Assessment
	What are your strengths? What are your weaknesses? If you were grading yourself based on this portfolio, what letter grade would you give yourself? Why?

Activity Buffet: Assessment

Assessment: Portfolio
Employment Portfolio Contents Checklist

Use this checklist as a guide when selecting the items that should be in your portfolio. You can also use it as the basis of your table of contents.

	Cover. Include key information (name, class, date); you may enhance it with graphics
	Title Page
	Table of Contents
	Introduction and Goals
	Employment Search
	Career Report: In-depth study of your first-choice career
	Student Career Plan
	Career Interest Survey Results/ASVAB Results
	Resume, Cover Letter, and Thank You Letter
	Mock Interview Evaluations
	Career Cluster Skill Samples
	Oral Communication Skills
	Written Communication Skills
	Math Skills
	Computer Skills
	Teamwork/Problem Solving Skills
	Skills Assessment
	Competency Assessment
	Classroom and Job Assessments
	Vocational Competency Assessment
	Work Experience
	Job Training Plan/Training Agreement
	Job Description (duties and tasks)
	Work Samples (if appropriate)
	Employer Job Skills Evaluation
	Transcripts
	High School
	Vocational School
	Vocational Certificate
	Accomplishments
	Honors and Awards (for example, attendance award)
	Community Activities
	School Activities
	Reference Letters
	Academic Teacher
	Counselor (optional)
	Vocational Teacher
	Employer

Activity Buffet: Assessment

Assessment: Portfolio
Rubric for Course Portfolio

Name____ **Date** _______________ **Period** _______

Course Portfolio Rubric		
Does Not Meet Expectations (0-1)	**Meets Expectations (2-3)**	**Exceeds Expectations (4-5)**
Format		
Cover or title page missing, Inappropriate folder or notebook	Every element present	Every element present and neat
Visual Appearance		
No creativity	Some creativity and design elements	Very creative with good use of design
Organization		
One or more portfolio items missing and/or turned in late	All items present, Turned in on time	All items present, Turned in on time, Extremely well organized
Knowledge		
No understanding	Understanding and some application	Good understanding and application
Grammar and Spelling		
Two or more errors	One error	No errors
Writing Style		
Not clear, Few marketing terms used or terms used incorrectly, Simple sentences, No or little logic	Reasonably clear, Uses some marketing terms correctly, Compound and complex sentences used, Logical development	Extremely clear, Uses many marketing terms correctly, Compound and complex sentences, Very logical development
Item Selection		
Poor choice	Reasonable choice	Excellent choice
Reflections		
One or more reflections missing, or reflections lack insight	Some insight	Very insightful

Total Points: _________ of 40

Comments: ____

____

____

____

Assessment: Portfolio
Rubric for Employment Portfolio

Name____ **Date** _____________ **Period** ______

Employment Portfolio Rubric		
Does Not Meet Expectations (0-1)	**Meets Expectations (2-3)**	**Exceeds Expectations (4-5)**
Format		
Cover or title page missing, Inappropriate folder or notebook, Sloppy	Every element present, Appropriate notebook or folder, Reasonably neat	Every element present, Appropriate notebook or folder, Very neat
Visual Appearance		
No creativity	Some creativity and design elements	Very creative with good use of design
Organization		
One or more portfolio items missing, Table of Contents missing, Turned in late	All items present, Table of Contents, Turned in on time	All items present, Table of Contents, Turned in on time, Extremely well organized
Writing Quality		
One or more errors in spelling or grammar, Writing unclear or lacking logical development	No errors in spelling or grammar, Writing reasonably clear and logical	No errors in spelling or grammar, Writing exceptionally clear and logical
Quality of Resume		
Resume poorly done	Solid resume	Excellent resume
Quality of Introduction and Goals, Career Cluster Skill Samples, and Work Experience Description		
One or more missing, Goals unclear, Poor examples or examples show poor skills, Work description weak	Clear goals, Solid examples and skills, Good work description	Clear goals, Excellent examples and skills, Excellent work description
Quality of Accomplishments		
No accomplishments	One solid accomplishment	One excellent or two or more solid accomplishments
Overall Impression		
Weak employability	Solid employability	Excellent employability

Total Points: _________ **of 40**

Comments: ____

____

____

____

____

Communication: Oral

Timers. Many of the speech suggestions set a time limit for speaking. If possible, get the type of timer that you can set on an overhead projector, so that all students can see the passage of time. Alternatively, choose someone to keep time (either you or a student) and have that person signal when 10 seconds are left and then call "time" when the time is up.

Persuasive Speech. Prepare a three-to-five minute speech. Choose a topic related to the chapter. Decide the goal of your speech. What do you want to persuade the listener to do? Possible topics include enroll in a marketing class, take a socially responsible action, become a member of a career and technical student organization, vote for a candidate. Write the speech, then practice delivering it.

Impromptu Speech. To get students comfortable with speaking in front of others, have them give impromptu speeches. Invite a student to the front of the class. Let the student choose any topic that he or she wants, and speak about it for two minutes. You might have one student speak a day until each student has had a chance. If it works well, continue having one student speak a day until the end of the term. As time goes on, you might suggest that students choose a topic from the current chapter about which to speak. Encourage students to clap for the speaker at the conclusion of each speech.

"Pick It Up From Here" Speech. The teacher or the first student chooses a topic. Topics can be from the current marketing chapter or a news item. Students might also be instructed to use vocabulary from the current chapter or chapters in the current part. The first student speaks for 30 seconds to one minute. Then the next student picks up from where the previous student ended and talks for another 30 seconds to one minute. Keep going around the class until everyone has spoken.

Give Directions. The teacher makes a list of locations in and around the school, such as the closest women's restroom, auditorium, or the culinary arts room. There should be as many destinations as students or teams in the class. The teacher assigns each location a number and writes each location and its number on a slip of paper. Each student or team draws a slip, and the teacher records which location and number each student or team drew. The students write the number of their location on a sheet of paper, and then write the directions for how to get to that location. Have each student orally give the location number and read the directions two or three times. The rest of the class writes down the location number and where the location is. Ask students to say the location. Count how many students named the correct location. That number is the score of the student who wrote/read the directions.

Another way to do this activity is to have students exchange directions so that no one has his or her own directions. Give students a day to use the directions to find their locations. Have students write their names and the location on the directions and turn them over to the teacher.

Guidelines for Writing and Speaking

Follow the **P-E-E-R** process for writing and speaking. It is often a good idea to write out a speech before you give it. Remember this: Writing is rewriting!

PLAN

- Who is your audience?
- What is your purpose or goal?
- What result do you want to see?
- What points do you want to cover?
- What format will be best?

EXECUTE

- Gather your sources.
- Make notes.
- Brainstorm ideas by writing them down or audiorecording all your ideas.
- Organize your ideas.
- Make an outline.
- Write.
- Practice giving a speech or an oral presentation.

EVALUATE

- Read over the speech for sense and clarity.
- Proofread for grammar and spelling.
- Try out the communication on a sample of your audience.
- Evaluate whether your goals have been met.

REVISE

- Use your evaluation to improve your writing or your speech.
- Use the feedback to adapt the message for your audience.
- Look over your revised message. Does the communication achieve your goal? If not, repeat the "Evaluate" and "Revise" steps until your communication achieves your goal.

Activity Buffet: Communication

Planning Form for Speaking and Writing

Name____ **Date** _____________ **Period** ______

Topic: ____

Title of Presentation: ____

Minutes Allotted for Presentation: ______________________________________

Decisions	Description
Topic	
Audience	
Purpose	
Desired Result	
Visuals (photos, diagrams, tables, charts)	
Equipment	
Format	
Sources	
Content (main points to cover)	

(Continue on another sheet if needed.)

Guidelines for Team Presentations

Many team activities conclude with a team presentation. The following guidelines will help your team prepare its presentation.

1. Have the team fill out the "Planning Form for Speaking and Writing."
2. Have the team list the tasks need to be completed.
3. Have the team discuss the strengths of each team member, then assign tasks to the member who is best qualified for each task.
4. Make sure each team member has a task.
5. Have team members complete their tasks.
6. Have the team practice its presentation.
7. Have team members make suggestions for improving the presentation.
8. Make improvements.
9. Practice again.
10. After the presentation is given, have team members discuss how well they did. Was the presentation successful? Was the audience interested?
11. Discuss the team process. Did the team decide by consensus or appoint a leader? Were there problems with decision making? Were the decisions good? How well did your team process work?

Activity Buffet: Communication

Evaluation: Individual Participation

Name____ **Date** _____________ **Period** _______

The rating scale below shows qualities of participation in class. On the scale, 1 is the lowest score; 5 is the best. Your score for each quality shows the level you have achieved, and what levels you can continue to try to reach. The total points indicate the overall quality of your participation.

Attentiveness				
1	2	3	4	5
Completely inattentive	Seldom attentive	Somewhat attentive	Usually attentive	Always attentive

Contribution to Discussion				
1	2	3	4	5
Never contributes	Rarely contributes	Occasionally contributes	Frequently contributes	Always contributes

Leadership				
1	2	3	4	5
Influences peers negatively	Does not follow leadership of other students	Follows leadership of other students	Sometimes assumes leadership role	Often assumes leadership and is respected by peers

Response to Teacher				
1	2	3	4	5
Unable to respond when called on	Occasionally answers questions	Usually answers questions, but seldom offers new ideas	Answers questions and occasionally offers new ideas with prompting	Answers questions and often offers new ideas without prompting

Total Points: _______ **of 20**

Comments: ____

____

____

____

Activity Buffet: Communication

Evaluation: Team Participation

Team Name ____ **Date** _____________ **Period** _______

Team Members: ____

____

____

____

The rating scale below shows qualities of team functioning. On the scale, 1 is the lowest score; 5 is the best. The score for each quality shows what the team as a whole has achieved and what the team can try to reach. Keep in mind your contribution to the team score. The total points indicate the overall quality of the team's functioning.

Teamwork				
1	2	3	4	5
Passive membership. Tasks not completed.	Argumentative membership. Members could not agree on who should do each task. Tasks not completed.	Independent membership. Members completed tasks individually and did not work together. Tasks completed.	Interactive membership. Members interacted, but had some difficulties working together. Tasks completed.	Cooperative membership. Members worked together smoothly and efficiently. All tasks completed.
Leadership				
1	2	3	4	5
No leadership established.	Competition for leadership led to no effective leadership.	Relied on outside source (e.g., the teacher) for leadership.	One member assumed primary leadership for the team.	Leadership responsibilities shared by several team members.
Goal Achievement				
1	2	3	4	5
Did not attempt to achieve goal.	Were unable to achieve goal.	Achieved goal with outside assistance.	Achieved goal.	Achieved goal with exceptional results.

Total Points: _______ **of 15**

These team members made excellent contributions to the group's efforts:

____

____

____

These team members failed to contribute to the group's efforts:

____

____

____

Activity Buffet: Communication

Evaluation: Oral Presentation

Name____ **Date** _____________ **Period** _______

Description of Assignment: ____

____

Title of Presentation: ____

____

Minutes Allotted for Presentation: ____

Criteria	Scale			
	Poor	**Fair**	**Good**	**Excellent**
Delivery				
Eye contact				
Gestures				
Voice volume				
Voice clarity				
Kept to time frame				
Content				
Topic focused				
Facts accurate				
Concrete examples				
Key information presented				
Organization				
Attention-grabbing opener				
Logical organization				
Easy to understand				
Summarizing close				
Visual Aids (if appropriate)				
Help understanding				
Provide interest				
Attractive				
Additional Criteria				

Comments: ____

____

____

Score/Grade:

Activity Buffet: Communication

Evaluation: Written Report

Name____ **Date** _____________ **Period** ______

Description of Assignment: ____

____

Title of Report:____

____

Due Date: ____

Criteria	Scale			
	Poor	**Fair**	**Good**	**Excellent**
Content				
Topic focused				
Facts accurate				
Concrete examples				
Key information presented				
Organization				
Attention-grabbing opener				
Logical organization				
Easy to understand				
Summarizing close				
Language Arts				
Grammar				
Spelling				
Format				
Neatness				
Clarity				
Style				
Visual Aids (if appropriate)				
Help understanding				
Provide interest				
Attractive				
Resources				
Uses references				
Cites references correctly				
Additional Criteria				

Comments: ____

____

____

Score/Grade:

Activity Buffet: Communication

Article Report

Name____ **Date** _______________ **Period** _______

Choose a topic from the chapter you are studying. Find a related article from a newspaper or magazine. You may instead type the topic into an Internet search engine, and find an article on the Internet.

Name of Newspaper, Magazine, or Web site: ____

____

Title of Article: ____

____

Author(s): ____

____

Date of Publication: ____

1. **Write a summary of the article, including how it relates to the chapter content.**_____________

____

____

____

____

____

2. **How will this information be useful to you now or in the future?** ______________________

____

____

____

____

3. **What is your opinion of this article?**____

____

____

____

____

4. **Would you recommend this article to others? Why or why not?**

____

____

____

____

Activity Buffet: Communication

Book Report

Name____ **Date** _____________ **Period** _______

Title of Book: ____

____

Author(s): ____

____

Publisher: ____

Copyright Date:____

1. **Why did you choose this book?** ____

____

____

____

2. **What key ideas did you learn?** ____

____

____

____

____

3. **What is your opinion of this book?**____

____

____

____

____

4. **Would you recommend this book to others? Why or why not?**

____

____

____

____

Field Trip Report

Name____ **Date** _______________ **Period** ________

Place Visited: ____

Location or Address:____

1. **What was the purpose of this field trip?** _______________________________________

   ____

   ____

2. **Summarize your field trip experience. Use as many marketing terms as possible.**

   ____

   ____

   ____

   ____

3. **What did you learn from this field trip?**____

   ____

   ____

   ____

   ____

4. **Would you recommend that other classes take this field trip? Answer yes or no, then explain your response.** ____

   ____

   ____

   ____

   ____

5. **Other comments:** ____

   ____

   ____

   ____

   ____

Activity Buffet: Communication

Guest Speaker Report

Name____ **Date** _____________ **Period** ______

Name of Speaker: ____

Speaker's Title: ____

Company Name: ____

1. **What was the purpose of inviting this guest to speak to the class?** _______________________

   ____

   ____

2. **Make a list of questions to ask the speaker.** ______________________________________

   ____

   ____

   ____

   ____

3. **What did you learn from this speech?** ____

   ____

   ____

   ____

   ____

4. **How will this information be useful to you now or in the future?** _____________________

   ____

   ____

   ____

5. **Were your questions answered? What else would you like to know from this speaker?**

   ____

   ____

   ____

   ____

Activity Buffet: Communication

Interview

Name_______________________________________ **Date** ______________ **Period** ______

Name of Interviewee: ____

Title or Position: ____

Address: ____

Phone: ____

Purpose of Interview: ____

Be sure to write a thank-you note to the interviewee after the interview!

Question 1: ____
____
____

Answer 1: ____
____
____
____
____

Question 2: ____
____
____

Answer 2: ____
____
____
____
____

Question 3: ____
____
____

Answer 3: ____
____
____
____

Activity Buffet: Communication

Reaction Paper

Name_______________________________________ **Date** _____________ **Period** _______

A reaction paper is an essay describing your response to something you read, a speech you heard, or an activity with which you were involved.

Identifying Information for Article, Speaker, or Activity:_______________________________

____

____

1. **Describe the article, speech, or activity.** _____________________________________

____

____

____

____

2. **What is your opinion of this article, speech, or activity?** ________________________

____

____

____

____

3. **What new ideas did you get?** ____

____

____

____

____

4. **How will this information be useful to you now or in the future?** ________________

____

____

____

____

5. **Would you recommend this article, speech, or activity to others? Why or why not?**

____

____

____

____

Activity Buffet: Content Review

Content Review: Individual or Group

Outline. Outline the chapter. Use the section headings as your outline headings. For each heading, write one or two sentences that summarize the main idea(s) under that heading.

Graphic Organizer. A graphic organizer is another way to outline a chapter. Make a circle in the middle of your paper. Write the chapter title inside. Then think, "How are the other concepts in the chapter related to this one?" Arrange these other ideas or concepts around the center one. Surround each idea with a circle. Connect these surrounding ideas to the center one with lines, in a way that shows the relationship among the ideas. You can use the major headings in the chapter as the ideas around the center one. Then look at each of the surrounding circles, and add the concepts that are related to them. Be sure to use all the terms in the chapter marketing terms list.

Main Concept. What is the main concept of this chapter? Describe it in a sentence. Then explain in writing why you think this concept is important. Describe where you might see examples of this concept in action in your daily life or on the job. Then describe how this concept might affect you, either in your life now or in the future. Use the words in the chapter marketing terms list.

Summary. Summarize the chapter in six to ten sentences.

Bulletin Board, Electronic Presentation, or Poster. Create a bulletin board, electronic presentation, or poster that presents the main concepts in the chapter. Find photos or draw diagrams to illustrate the concepts. Use the words in the marketing terms list.

Short Story. Write a short story. The story should have characters and a plot. Build the story around the concepts in the chapter. Use the words in the marketing terms list.

Poem, Rap, or Song. Write a poem, rap, or song. The subject is the concepts in this chapter. Use the words in the marketing terms list. Perform your poem, rap, or song for the class.

Dialog. Imagine that two characters in the work world are discussing the concepts in this chapter. Give each of your characters a name. Then write a dialog for them. In this dialog, they discuss the concepts in this chapter. Use the words in the marketing terms list. Perform the dialog with a partner.

Skit. Write a skit based on the concepts in this chapter. Use the words in the marketing terms list. Perform the skit for the class.

Nursery Rhyme. Find a nursery rhyme or other short, published work; and change the story to include information and terms from the chapter. Include a copy of the original work with title, author, and source.

Mnemonic. Have students create a memory sentence or words (mnemonic) to help them remember key concepts in the chapter. Have students share their mnemonics.

Content Review: Group

Quiz. Have students make up 5 to 15 questions for a quiz on this chapter. Students should use all the words in the marketing terms list as part of the questions or answers. Have students write the answers to their questions. Then, make a blank quiz. Have students put their names on their quizzes as the quiz writers. Have students exchange quizzes with a partner. Have them take the partner's quiz. Return the quiz to the quiz writer for correcting. Discuss the questions and the answers.

Look into the Microscope. Assign a chapter or specific pages from the text to read. After students have finished reading, have them write down as much as they can remember from the chapter. Give them five to ten minutes. Then, have students get into pairs. Each person tells the other what he or she remembers from the reading. Students may use their notes. They may also add to their notes if their partners tell them information that they did not remember. Then have two pairs join together, and have all members tell the others what they remember. You now have your class organized into four-member teams. These teams are now prepared for a Quiz Bowl competition.

Quiz Bowl. Quiz Bowl is an official DECA event and a fun way to review content. You can do this activity two ways: with and without a Quiz Bowl machine. Either way, have each student write five to eight questions with answers based on the chapter or chapters specified by the teacher. Put these questions into a bowl.

Without the Machine. Divide the class into two groups. The teacher is the moderator. Draw a question. Ask the first person in the first group the question. If this student does not answer correctly, invite the first person on the other team to answer. Continue in this way, switching teams whenever the team does not get the correct answer. End the game after a specific amount of time or when you run out of questions. The team with the most correct answers wins.

With the Machine. Purchase a Quiz Bowl machine. (One source of Quiz Bowl equipment is ZeeCraft-Tech at **zeecraft.com**). Follow the official Quiz Bowl guidelines, which you can get from DECA. You can also get official Quiz Bowl questions and answers from DECA. Organize your class into teams of four. The team that answers the most questions correctly will continue to compete against another team who has not participated. You may want to award certificates to the winning teams.

Activity Buffet: Decision Making and Ethics

Decision-Making Worksheet

Consult your textbook, Chapter 5, Figure 5-7, "Steps in Ethical Decision Making" for a description of each step. Then write your situation and process for each step.

Ethical Decision-Making Worksheet	
1. State the problem.	
2. Gather information.	
3. List options.	
4. Evaluate options.	
5. Consider ethical implications.	
6. Make a decision.	
7. Implement the decision.	
8. Evaluate results.	

Activity Buffet: Decision Making and Ethics

DECA Five-Step Decision-Making Process

DECA Decision-Making Worksheet

1. State the problem. Use one sentence to describe the problem.	
2. Identify all the important facts. Go over the facts. Make sure that you are *not* considering hearsay or rumors as facts.	
3. List all the possible solutions to the problem. Make sure to include positive and negative solutions. You might think firing an employee is a negative solution; however, it may be a positive solution.	
4. List the results of each possible solution. Although this part of the decision making process is time-consuming, this step will force you to see both the positive and negative results of each possible solution.	
5. Choose the best possible solution. Your solution should be the best way to solve the problem that you identified in step #1. It should also be based on thorough analysis of the facts and options.	

Activity Buffet: Decision Making and Ethics

Three-Step Ethical Decision-Making Process

Here is a three-step ethical process, described by Kenneth H. Blanchard and Norman Vincent Peale in their book, *The Power of Ethical Management.*

Three-Step Ethical Decision-Making Worksheet	
Is it legal?	
Is it balanced?	
How would I feel if my name were on the front page of the newspaper for everyone to see?	

Activity Buffet: Decision Making and Ethics

Ethical Challenges

It's Questionable. Describe examples of questionable and possibly unethical behaviors.

Be a Star. Create a script and act out unethical (but not illegal) behaviors that might occur at work or school.

How Do You Change? Why do people choose to be unethical? Make a list of unethical behaviors or situations that occur at school or work. Then explain what could be done to discourage unethical behavior or help people change to ethical behavior.

Ethical Adjectives. List adjectives that describe ethical behavior.

Unethical Adjectives. List adjectives that describe unethical behavior.

Statement of Ethics. Compose your personal statement of ethics.

Ethical Challenges Scenarios. Organize students into groups. Have each group write a scenario that presents an ethical dilemma, either at work or at school. Then give all students one of the decision-making worksheets, and have them analyze the situation and make a decision. Have the group discuss each group member's decision. Have the group vote on the best one. Then have each group present their scenario and decision.

Read *The Power of Ethical Management* by Kenneth H. Blanchard and Norman Vincent Peale. Write a summary of the book.

Read from *The Power of Ethical Management,* the Man in the Glass, found on pages 44 – 45. With the class or in small groups, discuss what this means to them as individuals.

Interview a Businessperson. Interview a manager or business owner about ethics at work. Compose questions prior to the interview. Have these questions approved by your instructor before the interview. Compose a written report or schedule a time to present an oral report to the class.

Ethics at the School Store. Have students list unethical behaviors that they have observed or committed at the school store. Then have students describe how these behaviors should be handled and what can be done to discourage these behaviors before they occur.

Guest Speaker. Invite a speaker on the topic of ethical and unethical behavior.

Internet Search. Use a search engine to locate three articles on the Internet about ethical and unethical behavior. Read the articles and write a summary of each.

Storytime. Have students write stories that involve three or more people in ethical and unethical situations. The stories should be at least four paragraphs long. Have students trade stories and identify the ethical and unethical behaviors.

Ethics in the News. Have students search newspapers, magazines, and the Internet for recent stories of unethical business behavior. Have students present the situations and results to the class. Then post the articles on a bulletin board.

Debate. Take one of the recent ethical situations in the news. Organize the class into groups of four. In each group, two will debate the pro side and two will debate the con side. Give groups time to research support for their sides. Have small groups hold their debates. Then ask a group to volunteer to debate in front of the class. Have the class vote on which side was ethical.

Activity Buffet: Decision Making and Ethics

Quotes and Sayings for Ethical Inspiration

Ask students to explain what each quote or saying means. You could also ask them to describe a situation to which the quote or saying can be applied, and then explain how the quote or saying applies. You could also ask them to research the author of the quote, briefly describe the person's life, and tell why or give the context in which the person said the quoted material. For additional quotations and sayings, enter "Quotations" and "ethics" into an Internet search engine.

"There is no pillow as soft as a clear conscience." John Wooden

"It is hard for an empty bag to stand upright." Benjamin Franklin

"There is no right way to do the wrong thing." Thomas Huxley

"It is often easier to fight for principles than live up to them." Adlai Stevenson

"Live together like brothers and do business like strangers." Anonymous

"One must care about a world one will not see." Bertrand Russell

"No and Yes are words quickly said, but they need a great amount of thought before you utter them." Baltasar Gracián

"If you think about what you ought to do for other people, your character will take care of itself." Woodrow Wilson

"If it is not right, do not do it; if it is not true do not say it." Marcus Aurelius

"In looking for people to hire, you look for three qualities: integrity, intelligence, and energy. And if they don't have the first, the other two will kill you." Warren Buffet

"To be persuasive, we must be believable; to be believable we must be credible; to be credible, we must be truthful." Edward R. Murrow

"People are going to want, and be able, to find out about the citizenship of a brand, whether it is doing the right things socially, economically, and environmentally." Mike Clasper

"Integrity is the essence of everything successful." Buckminster Fuller

"The time is always right to do what is right." Martin Luther King, Jr.

"If we do not change our direction, we are likely to end up where we are headed." Chinese Proverb

"It takes 20 years to build a reputation and five minutes to ruin it." Warren Buffet.

"Corporate social responsibility is a hard-edged business decision. Not because it is a nice thing to do or because people are forcing us to do it . . . because it is good for our business." Niall Fitzerald

"Corporate social responsibility is not just about managing, reducing, and avoiding risk; it is about creating opportunities, generating improved performance, making money, and leaving the risks far behind." Sunil Misser

Activity Buffet: Games

Game Instructions

Game Slips. Many games and activities use terms written on slips of paper. Use the "Game Slips" reproducible in this section to make your slips.

MARKO. Give each student a MARKO board. Give students a list of terms, for example, the "Marketing Terms" list at the beginning of a chapter, or the list of types of utilities, or the list of the functions of marketing, or any other similar list of information the students should know. The list of terms can also be the answers to a predetermined list of questions. If there are more boxes than terms, students can use the terms more than once. Have students fill in their MARKO boards by writing the terms in the boxes, in random order. You, the teacher, then read a list of questions to which the terms are answers, or a list of definitions for the terms. Give each question or definition a number, and read that number along with the question or definition. This is so that you can check the students' answers.

Students look for the answer on their MARKO boards, then write the question/definition number in the appropriate box. As in Bingo, a person has MARKO when the MARKO board boxes are covered in the four corners, horizontally, vertically, or diagonally. Have students yell out "Marko!" then have the student read the number, the definition or question, and the answer for each MARKO item. If all are correct, the student wins.

Tic/Tac/Mark. Give each student a "Tic/Tac/Mark" board. Give students a list of terms, for example, the "Marketing Terms" list at the beginning of a chapter, or the list of types of utilities, or the list of the functions of marketing. The list of terms can also be the answers to a predetermined list of questions. If there are more boxes than terms, students can use the terms more than once. Have students fill in their Tic/Tac/Mark boards by writing the terms in the boxes, in random order. You, the teacher, then read a list of questions to which the terms are answers, or a list of definitions for the terms. Give each question or definition a number, and read that number along with the question or definition. This is so that you can check the students' answers.

Students look for the answer on their Tic/Tac/Mark board, then write the question/definition number in the appropriate box. As in Tic/Tac/Toe, a person has Tic/Tac/Mark when the board boxes are covered in a row horizontally, vertically, or diagonally. Have students yell out "Tic/Tac/Mark!" then have the student read the number, the definition or question, and the answer for each item. If all are correct, the student wins.

Charades. Select a category of terms that students should know, such as marketing functions, utilities, types of promotion, and so on. Create a set of terms in the category on slips of paper. Place the terms in an envelope or bowl. Ask a volunteer to draw a slip and act out the term. Tell the class the category of terms. Have the class guess the term.

Twenty Questions. Choose a category of terms that students should know, such as types of business customers, utilities, or types of promotion. Create enough slips with these terms on them for about a third of the class. (You will probably have the same term two or three times.) Create enough blank slips for the rest of the class. Place all the slips in an envelope or bowl. Have each student draw a slip. Ask all the students who have drawn terms to come to the front of the classroom. The rest of the class (the students who drew the blank slips) takes turns asking "yes/no" questions of each person who drew a term. When a student gets a "yes" answer, he or she can guess the term. For every "yes" response, the student gets one point. The student with the most points will be the official winner, and you may award a prize.

Trivia. Have each student develop trivia question/answer cards for a specific marketing activity, for example, the topic of the current chapter. Give students time to research additional information that others might not know. Have each student, in turn, read his or her question. For each question that the class cannot answer, award one point to the questioner. The student who accumulates the most points can be declared the winner and may be awarded a prize.

Activity Buffet: Games

Game Slips

Use this form when you need to make slips of paper for a game.

Activity Buffet: Games

MARKO

Your teacher will give you a list of terms or phrases. Write one term or phrase in each blank in the MARKO board. The order should be random. This game is similar to Bingo.

M	A	R	K	O
		FREE SPOT		

Tic/Tac/Mark

Your teacher will give you a list of terms or phrases. Write one term or phrase in each blank in the Tic/Tac/Mark board. The order should be random. This game is similar to Tic/Tac/Toe.

Getting to Know You

I'd Like You to Meet . . . . Organize students into pairs. Tell students that the goal is to have each person introduce his or her partner, so that the class members can learn something about their classmates and write their names on their seating charts. They are to learn and share the following information about their partners: full name, nickname or preferred name (if appropriate), where they work if they work, which grade they are in (if it is a multigrade class), what school they are from (if it is a center with students from several schools), and a hobby or favorite book, movie, song, or band. Give students about four minutes, two apiece, to learn the information.

Have each student introduce his or her partner. If you (the teacher) have partnered with a student, you and your partner should go first. Write the name and preferred name of each student on your overhead seating chart. Have students do the same on their copies of the seating chart.

What's in a Name? Organize the class into pairs. Have each person ask the other about his or her name. Why were they given that name? Do they have a preferred nickname? How did they get it? Give students about two to four minutes to ask questions and be prepared to introduce the other person.

Birthday Game. Have students get up out of their seats. Tell them that they cannot use any spoken words to communicate. They also cannot write any words to communicate. Then tell them to put themselves in order by birthday. When the class is done, have each student say his or her birthday. Then discuss how difficult it was to communicate nonverbally. You might expand the discussion to communication in general and what methods they used to communicate nonverbally.

MARKO Scavenger Hunt. Ahead of time, prepare MARKO boards. In each square, place something that students are likely to have done over the summer, such as visited Florida, played tennis, went to a wedding, drove a foreign car. MARKO boards can be different for each student. Tell students that their goal is to find at least one student who has done each activity in each square. When they find a student, he or she should sign the square on the MARKO board. When a student has filled in the board with signatures, he or she can yell "MARKO." You can conclude the scavenger hunt then, or let everyone finish and give a prize to the student who finished first. To help the students remember each other, have the student who finished first read out loud the names of the students for each square.

Activity Buffet: Getting to Know You

Who Is Dynamic?

Circulate through the room to find members of the class who have the interests that are listed below. When you locate a match, ask the person his or her name, then record the name on the blank next to the statement. You may have more than one person's name on a line. You may also have a person's name more then once on the sheet. Make sure you talk with everyone! Have a dynamic time! When you have at least one name on each line, you may be seated.

Likes to draw:____

Enjoys science class: ____

Likes to sing: ____

Enjoys participating in sports: _______________________________

Likes to write: ____

Likes to investigate: ____

Enjoys working on the computer: _____________________________

Plays a musical instrument: __________________________________

Likes math:____

Enjoys selling products: _____________________________________

Likes to exercise: ____

Enjoys caring for animals: ___________________________________

Likes history: ____

Enjoys teaching others: _____________________________________

Likes to be creative: ____

Enjoys helping people:_______________________________________

Likes being around children: _________________________________

Likes to travel: ____

Likes to read: ____

Likes to design fashions: ____________________________________

Likes to build things:____

Likes to shop: ____

Enjoys making money:_______________________________________

Activity Buffet: Getting to Know You

Box Factory
Teacher Guidelines

Purpose of Activity

- Students experience how to communicate nonverbally.
- Students experience teamwork.

Materials

- Unlimited amount of white paper, 8½ by 11 inches
- Two pairs of scissors per group
- Two glue sticks or tape dispensers per group
- Two pencils per group

Preparation

- For each student, a copy of the Box Factory worksheet and Box template.

Procedure

1. Organize students into teams of five to seven.
2. Tell students that their team is to make as many perfectly formed boxes as possible in ten minutes, but they are not allowed to speak to each other.
3. If you wish, you can assign one person in each team to observe and make sure no one talks during the activity. Each team is allowed only one lapse. If the silence is broken more than once, the team is disqualified.
4. While teams are working, walk around and observe how well the teams are working together and dealing with the "no speaking" rule.
5. If students have trouble figuring out how to make the boxes, stop the activity, do a demonstration, then have them start again.
6. After ten minutes, the teacher will perform quality control. You may set any criteria that you wish to determine which boxes are approved and counted. Tell each group the number of approved boxes to note on their worksheets.
7. Have students complete their worksheets, then hold a discussion.

Alternate Procedures

1. After five minutes of box production, have all teams stop. Tell them that they are allowed to talk for the remaining five minutes of production.
2. After five minutes of box production, have all teams stop. Have everyone watch as you perform quality control on each team's boxes. Tell each team how many acceptable boxes it has. Then have teams continue making boxes for five more minutes. See if any teams change production methods to better meet the needs of the customer (you).

(Continued)

3. Either after five minutes, or in a new box-making session, have students draw slips with different attitudes or personal qualities to portray. Ahead of time create slips with a variety of the following: positive/optimistic attitudes (such as friendly, talkative, smiling), negative/pessimistic attitudes (such as angry, uncooperative, frowning), leadership styles (such as autocratic or democratic), and personality traits (such as indifferent or domineering).

Discussion Questions

1. How difficult was it to complete the boxes without talking?
2. How did you communicate?
3. Which methods of nonverbal communication were most effective?
4. How effective was your team?
5. What would help improve the effectiveness of your team?

Questions for Alternate Procedures

1. How did production change when you were allowed to talk?
2. Was there more or less teamwork with or without talking?
3. Did your team complete more boxes when you were allowed to talk with each other?
4. How did being able to talk affect the quality of your boxes?
5. How did observing the quality control help you improve your quality?
6. How did the different attitudes of the team members affect your productivity and quality?

Time Frame

This activity is designed to be completed in one class period of 40 to 50 minutes; however, it can take longer depending on whether you do the alternate procedures and how well your students follow directions. Allow five minutes to present the activity and distribute materials, ten minutes for making boxes, ten minutes for the teacher to perform quality control and count the boxes, and five minutes for discussion.

Activity Buffet: Getting to Know You

Box Factory

Name_______________________________________ **Date** _____________ **Period** _______

Words to Know

efficiency. Degree to which something is produced without waste of time or materials.
productivity. Amount of product a worker produces in a specified time period, such as amount/hour.
quality. The level of excellent in something.

Procedure

1. You will be assigned to a team.
2. Your team will make as many perfectly formed boxes as possible.
3. Use the box template on the back of this page.
4. Each team will get two pairs of scissors, two glue sticks or tape dispensers, and two pencils.
5. You will have an unlimited supply of box material (white paper).
6. You will have ten minutes to make your boxes, but you will not be allowed to talk to each other.
7. When time is up, the teacher will perform a quality control check and tell you how many boxes are acceptable.

Questions to Answer

1. How many boxes did your team produce? ____

2. Evaluate the quality of your boxes. ____

   ____

3. Did your group choose a leader? Why or why not? _________________________________

   ____

4. Did each team member make complete boxes, or did you divide up the tasks (specialize)?

   ____

5. How did you communicate? ____

   ____

6. What strategies did the winning team use? _______________________________________

   ____

7. How could you improve the efficiency of your team? _______________________________

   ____

Activity Buffet: Getting to Know You

Box Template

DIRECTIONS: Cut on solid lines, and fold on dotted lines.

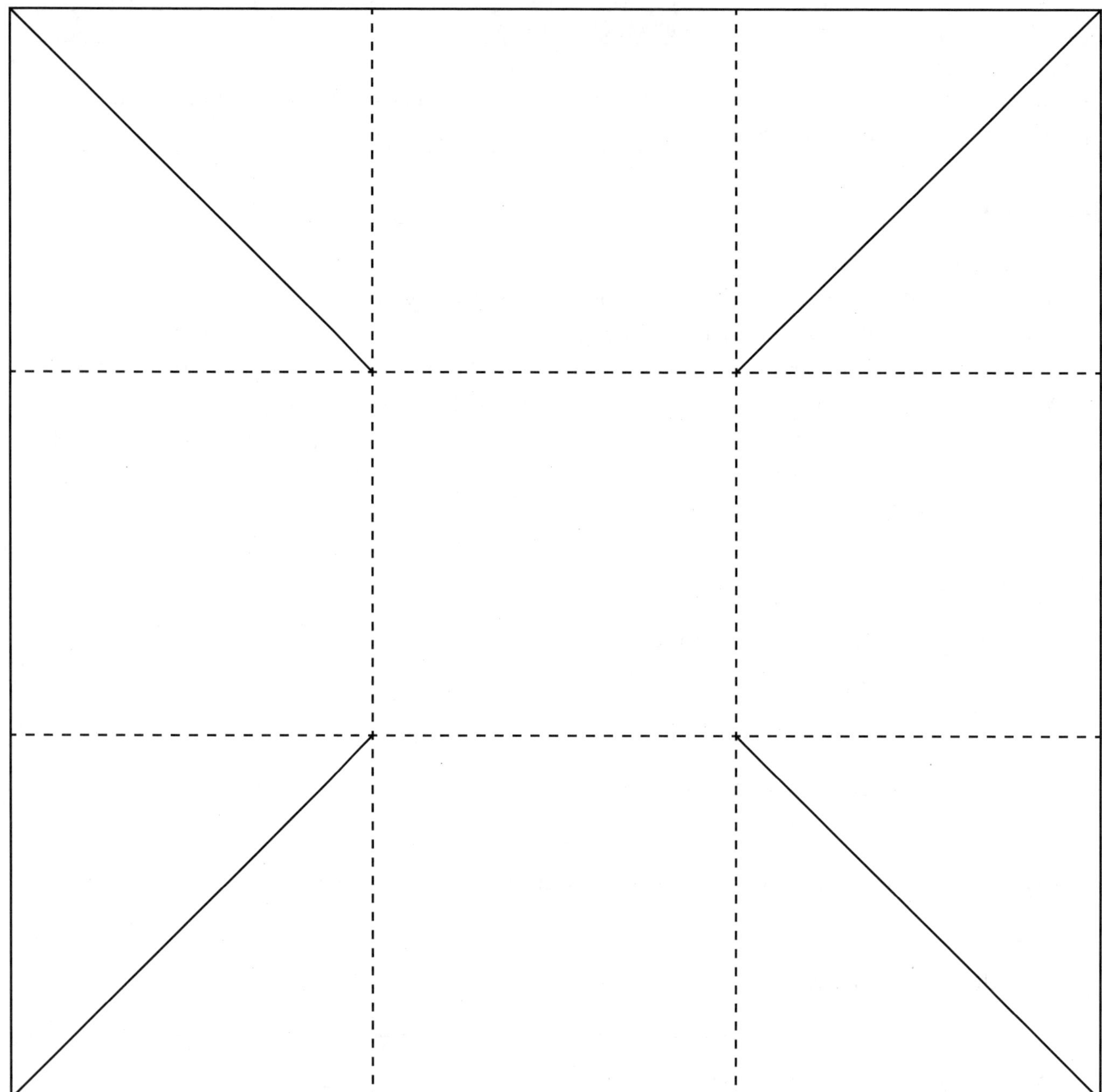

Parliamentary Procedure in Brief

Parliamentary procedure is based on *Robert's Rules of Order,* originally published in 1896. Consult the most recent edition for detailed guidelines.

Purpose

The purpose of parliamentary procedures is to protect the right of the majority to decide, the right of the minority to be heard, and the rights of individual members. Parliamentary procedure is designed to help, not hinder, group decision making.

Foundation

The foundation of parliamentary procedure is that all members of the group are equal and their rights are equal. Each member has the right to attend meetings, make motions, speak in debate, nominate, vote, and hold office.

Key Rules

A quorum must be present to conduct business. A *quorum* is the number (or percent) of the membership that must be present to legally conduct business. The number or percent that constitutes a quorum is usually stated in the organization's bylaws. The purpose of requiring a quorum is to prevent a small group from taking over and acting on behalf of the whole organization.

The majority rules. Everyone should be heard. However, once a decision has been made by the majority, everyone must abide by the decision.

One question and one speaker at a time.

Personal remarks are always out of order. All remarks should concern the motion, not the personalities of people sponsoring the motion.

How a Motion Is Made and Acted Upon

1. A member requests the floor.
2. Chair recognizes member.
3. Motion is stated, in the form, "I move that . . . ."
4. Motion is seconded.
5. Chair states the motion.
6. Debate of motion.
7. Chair puts the question to a vote.
8. Chair announces the vote.

Activity Buffet: Parliamentary Procedure

Terms Used in Parliamentary Procedure

adjourn. To end a meeting.

agenda. A list of things to be done and discussed at a meeting.

amend the motion. To change the wording of a motion that has been made.

aye. The formal term for *yes* (pronounced *eye*).

bylaws. The rules and regulations that govern an organization.

chair. The presiding officer at a meeting, such as the president or chairperson.

committee. A groups of members selected to perform a specific task.

debate. To speak *for* or *against* a motion. Every member of the organization has a right to debate an issue.

general consent. To accept a motion without a vote.

have the floor. Have the right to speak in a meeting without interruption from others.

in order. Relevant to the business being discussed.

majority. At least one more than half the members present at the meeting.

minutes. A written record of the business covered at a meeting.

motion. A recommendation by a member that a certain action be taken by the group.

nay. The formal term for *no.*

out of order. Not relevant to the business at hand, or in violation of one of the rules of order.

question. Another term for a motion.

quorum. The number of members who must be present to legally conduct business at a meeting. The number or percent of the membership is usually stated in the bylaws.

Robert's Rules of Order. The original manual of rules for parliamentary procedure, published in 1896. It has been revised and updated regularly. Consult the most recent edition for a complete discussion of parliamentary procedure.

roll call. Reading the name of each member to obtain and record his or her vote on a motion.

second the motion. The approval of a motion by another member.

table the motion. To delay making a decision on a motion.

voting. The process by which the decision of each member on a motion is expressed and recorded. Motions that are likely to be passed can be voted on by voice, a show of hands, or general consent. If the vote is likely to be close or a record of each person's vote is necessary, the vote can be done by role call. If secrecy is needed, the vote can be done by ballot.

Tips for Effective Meetings

Have an Agenda

An *agenda* is a list of topics to be discussed, decisions to be made, or other goals for a meeting. See sample agenda on a separate sheet.

Presiding Officer Should Keep Control

The role of the presiding officer is critical. This person has the responsibility to get the meeting started on time and focused on the agenda items. It is also the presiding officer's responsibility to make sure all key issues are addressed and votes are taken. The presiding officer must also make sure all the Robert's Rules of Order are followed. Here are some suggestions for the presiding officer:

- Be on time and start the meeting on time.
- Be organized. Have an agenda and stick to it.
- Be prepared. Know the rules of parliamentary procedure.
- Be in control of the meeting. Know how to properly and politely focus the discussion and move motions to vote.
- Be impartial and fair.
- Be precise. Always restate motion before taking a vote.

Write Minutes

Minutes are an essential part of any organization. Minutes are the official, legal record of what decisions were made at each meeting. The presiding officer should make sure that someone takes minutes at each meeting and formally submits them afterward. Minutes should include the following items:

- Name of organization
- Date and place of meeting
- Time of meeting
- Number of members present and whether the quorum was met
- Whether the minutes from previous meeting were approved or corrected
- Exact wording of all adopted and defeated motions
- Name of the maker of each motion
- Names of all officers and members who made a report
- Names of those elected or appointed

Activity Buffet: Parliamentary Procedure

Sample Agenda for a DECA Chapter Meeting

- Call to Order
- Opening Ceremonies
  Welcoming Remarks
  Invocation (Optional)
  Pledge of Allegiance
- Minutes of the Previous Meeting
- Reports of Officers
  Report of the Treasurer
- Report of the Executive Board
  (Annual Meeting)
- Reports of the Standing Committees
- Reports of the Special Committees
- Unfinished Business
  (Do not use the term "old" business.)
- New Business
- Program
- Announcements
- Adjournment

Activity Buffet: Reading

Why a Race Car?
Teacher Guidelines

Your students are members of the Millennial generation, that is, people born between 1982 and 2002. Many of these students do not like to read and have no interest in their textbooks. As high school marketing teachers, one of our jobs is to stimulate interest in both marketing and reading about marketing. Your first opportunity to do this occurs when you introduce students to their *Marketing Dynamics* textbook.

Hand out the textbook to students. Ask them *not* to open it. Organize students into pairs or small groups. Have them brainstorm what they think the book will be about. Have groups share their ideas with the whole class. Record their ideas on an overhead or easel.

Further Discussion Questions

- Why is the word "dynamics" in the title? What does "dynamic" mean? What are "dynamics"? Name some items or people whom you would describe as dynamic. (Dynamic *means energetic, forceful, characterized by productive activity or change.)*

- What is marketing? (*Accept all answers. Say that you will learn more about what marketing is when you begin to read the text.)*

- Why is a race car on the cover? (*There are a variety of answers. Race cars are fast-paced, and so is marketing. Race car drivers strive to stay ahead of their competition, and marketers also strive to stay ahead of their competition. NASCAR has done an excellent job of changing its image and marketing itself to a broad range of customers.)*

- Why is the Lowe's logo on the car? (*Lowe's, a company that sells home improvement products and supplies, sponsors this race car and its driver. Lowe's wants people to know that it sponsors this race car.)*

- Why would a company like Lowe's want the logo of its store on a race car? (*Millions of people watch NASCAR races. Those millions of people will see the Lowe's logo on this car. Seeing the Lowe's logo may make people happy that they already shop at Lowe's. In addition, seeing the logo may influence others to begin shopping at Lowe's.)*

Have students turn to the back cover of the book. Organize students into pairs or groups. Have the groups answer these questions: What does the photo show? Why do you think this photo was chosen? What are the four large words on the back cover? Why do you think they are there?

Have groups share their answers with the class.

Activity Buffet: Reading

What's in My Textbook?

Name____ **Date** ______________ **Period** ________

Follow the instructions below and answer the questions.

1. **Find the title page of the book.** What is the title of the book? ________________________________

   ____

2. **Who are the authors of the book and where are they from?** ________________________________

   ____

   ____

   ____

   ____

3. **Who are the contributing writers of the book and where are they from?** ____________________

   ____

   ____

   ____

4. **Name the publisher of the book.** ____

5. **Find "Introduction."** What does the information on this page tell you? ____________________

   ____

6. **Find "About the Authors."** In what way is each author/writer qualified to write this book?

   ____

   ____

   ____

7. **Find "Reviewers."** Why do you think the authors and publisher consulted these reviewers?

   ____

   ____

   ____

8. **Find "Brief Contents" and "Contents."** What is the difference between "Brief Contents" and "Contents"? Why do you think both are included? ____

   ____

   ____

   ____

9. **Into how many parts is the text divided?** ____

(*Continued*)

Name____ **Date** _____________ **Period** ______

10. **How many chapters are in the book?** ____

11. **List two topics from "Contents" that catch your interest.**

____

____

12. **Find each part opener.** Describe the main topic of each part.

____

____

____

____

____

____

____

____

____

13. **Look through the text.** Find a photograph that you really like. Write down the figure number and page number. Then describe the photo and explain why you like it. _______________________

____

____

14. **What information is on the first page of each chapter?**________________________________

____

____

15. **What is at the end of each chapter?** ____

16. **Which sections of the *Chapter Review* help you learn content?**

____

____

____

17. **Which sections of the *Chapter Review* help you expand your knowledge and prepare for the future?** ____

____

____

____

(Continued)

Name____ **Date** _______________ **Period** _______

18. What does the text do to help you learn new terms? _______________________________________

____

____

____

19. Find one of the profiles. Why do you think this person or organization was included in the book? _______________________________________

____

____

____

20. Find the glossary. How might you use the glossary?_______________________________________

____

____

____

21. Find the index. How might you use the index? ____

____

____

____

SQ3R

Student Instructions

SQ3R is the acronym for a method of reading and study first developed by F. P. Robinson. Many students find that this method helps them learn and remember what they have learned. The acronym stands for **S**urvey, **Q**uestion, **R**ead, **R**ecite, **R**eview. Before you use SQ3R, obtain or make copies of the SQ3R Worksheet. Note the chapter number and title.

Survey

Before you start reading, prepare yourself for the material you are reading. Survey the material you plan to read. For example, if you plan to read a chapter in *Marketing Dynamics,* survey it by doing the following: (1) Read the chapter title, Marketing Terms list, and list of objectives on the first page of the chapter. (2) Read the Reality Checks and headings within the chapter. (3) Look at the illustrations and read the captions. (4) Read "Remember This" and "Review Concepts" questions in the Chapter Review.

Question

After doing the survey, what questions do you have about the topic of the chapter? Write these questions in the "Question" column of the SQ3R Worksheet. If no questions come to mind, turn each heading in the chapter into a question. Begin questions with words such as *who, what, where, when, how, list,* or *name.* Asking questions sets the purpose for your reading. The purpose for your reading is to find answers to these questions.

Read

Read the chapter. As you find the answers to your questions, write the answers in the "Notes" column of your SQ3R Worksheet. Feel free to add questions to the Questions column if new questions arise while reading.

Recite

After you have read the chapter, look at the SQ3R Worksheet. Cover up the notes, so that just the questions appear. Ask yourself each question, then say or write the answer. Check your answers to make sure they are correct by rereading the text or your notes. Do the same for any question you could not answer. Reciting the answers in this way helps you correct any errors and remember the correct information. Answering these questions also helps you prepare for quizzes and tests.

Review

About a day after completing the recite step, review the questions and answers. Repeat the recite step. Reflect on how this chapter fits in with the other chapters you have studied. Reflect on how the information in this chapter will be useful to you in the future. Repeat the review step as often as you need to. More reviewing helps you remember the information better and longer.

Activity Buffet: Reading

SQ3R Worksheet

Name____ **Date** _____________ **Period** ______

Name of Text: *Marketing Dynamics*	
Chapter Number and Title:	
Questions	**Notes**

Prereading Activities

Assessing prior knowledge. Write the topic of the lesson or chapter on the board or an overhead. Ask students to take a piece of notebook paper and write everything they know about the topic. Let students write for about five minutes. Collect what students have written. If you see that most students do not have sufficient background knowledge for a topic, plan an activity that will provide more background, such as a hands-on activity, guest speaker, film, video, or field trip.

What do you know? When you enter the classroom, write the topic of study on the blackboard or easel pad. Have students go up to the board or easel and write down what they know about the topic. Discuss with the class.

What do you want to know? Have students look at the photos in the chapter and quickly read the main headings and figure captions. Have them write three questions or things they want to know about the chapter topic. Have students share their questions. As a group, set the purpose for reading the chapter and studying the topic.

How will you learn what you want to know? After students have listed three questions or things they want to know, ask them to describe how they can find the answers.

PreP. This prereading plan, developed by J.A. Langer in 1981, has three steps:

1. *Associations.* Choose a key word or phrase from the topic of the lesson or chapter. Say to the class, "Tell me what you think of when I say . . . ." For example, "Tell me what you think of when I say *advertising*." As each student tells you, write the response on the board, overhead, or easel pad. For example, a student might say, "Newspapers."

2. *Reflections.* Ask students, "What made you think of . . . [the student's association]." For example, the teacher asks, "What made you think of newspapers?" The student answers, "I see lots of ads in the newspaper."

3. *New Ideas.* Ask students, "Now that we have discussed the topic, do you have any new or more detailed ideas about the topic? Now what do you think of when I say . . . ?" For example, the teacher asks, "What do you think of now when I say *advertising*?" The student answers, "A way to inform people about a product."

Anticipation guide. This prereading activity, developed by J. E. Readance in 1986, encourages students to make predictions based on their prior knowledge, then read with purpose to test their predictions.

1. Look through the chapter to be read. Look for key concepts. Write five to ten statements, some accurate and some inaccurate. The inaccurate ones can be based on misconceptions that the students may have.

2. Students can respond either in writing or in a whole group discussion. In writing, prepare handouts with the statements listed down the page, and two columns next to the list of statements. See "Anticipation Guide Form." The first column is labeled "Before Reading." The second column is labeled "After Reading." Have students read each statement, then write "yes or no" or "agree or disagree" in the first column.

3. In a whole group discussion, read each statement. Have students indicate thumbs up or thumbs down. Then discuss.

Have students predict what the chapter will be about.

4. Have students read the text, then revisit each statement and respond based on what they have learned from their reading. Have students describe what they have learned from the chapter.

Activity Buffet: Reading

Anticipation Guide Form

Before Reading	Statements	After Reading

Predict what the chapter will be about.

____

____

____

After reading, write what you learned from your reading.

____

____

____

____

____

KWL
Teacher Guidelines

The KWL reading strategy was developed by Donna Ogle in 1986. It is an organized approach to prereading, during reading, and after reading activities. It helps students learn how to be actively involved in their reading.

The abbreviation stands for **K**now, **W**ant to know, and **L**earned. When first using this strategy, do it as a whole class activity. Also, choose a topic with which the students have some familiarity. Choose a short section of text that the students can read in class. When students become more familiar with the KWL strategy, they can do it on their own. When you assign students a chapter to read as homework, you can require that they turn in their own KWL charts and summary of the reading.

In-Class KWL Procedure

1. Make a large chart on an overhead, board, or easel pad. The title of the chart is the topic of the chapter (or part of a chapter) to be read. The chart has three columns. The first is labeled "K—What We Know." The second is labeled "W—What We Want to Know." The third is labeled "L—What We Learned." When students make this chart on their own as homework or seatwork, substitute "I" for "We."

Topic or Chapter Number and Title		
K—What We Know	**W— What We Want to Know**	**L— What We Learned**

2. Before students read the text, ask, "What do you know about this topic?" Record their answers in the first column (K). If students have trouble thinking of things they know, ask them what other words come to mind when you read the topic or chapter title to them.

3. After you have recorded what they already know, ask, "What else would you like to know about this topic?" The first time you do this, you may have to model a question for them. Record all their questions in the second column (W). When you have a decent list of questions, go through the list. You might ask a different student to read each of the questions.

4. Now tell students to read the section of text, while keeping these questions in mind. Tell them that when they find an answer to one of the questions, to write the answer on a piece of paper. If they think of any new questions, they should write the new questions also. Give students sufficient class time to read the section and write answers and new questions.

5. When students have completed reading and writing, have a class discussion. Ask, "What did you learn from the reading? Did you find the answers to the questions in the W column?" As students reply, record their answers in the third column (L).

6. After you have recorded everything the students learned in the L column, have each student write a summary of the reading and turn it in. Review students' summaries to determine how well they are learning the strategy and the content. Use students' summaries as a basis for reteaching and reinforcing the KWL strategy and topic content.

7. To reinforce content, have each student create a graphic organizer to help him or her remember the content.

8. To extend learning, after students have written their summaries, ask, "What else do you want to know about this topic? Where could you find this information?" Make a new list of questions. As appropriate, assign students or student groups a question to explore further. Students can present the results of their research as a written report, oral presentation, poster, or electronic presentation.

Activity Buffet: Reading

Questions to Ask While Reading

This page is a master for making four bookmarks. Copy this page onto paper or card stock. Cut apart. Make enough to give one bookmark to each student. When you give them to students, tell them to use these bookmarks when reading their textbook. After they have read a paragraph or two, they should stop and ask themselves the questions on the bookmark and answer them. Demonstrate how to use the bookmarks: Read a paragraph out loud to the class, then model how to ask and answer the questions. Then have students read another paragraph to themselves. Then call on students to demonstrate how to ask and answer the questions on the bookmarks. Suggest that students ask themselves these questions whenever they read the text.

Questions to Ask While Reading	**Questions to Ask While Reading**	**Questions to Ask While Reading**	**Questions to Ask While Reading**
Do I understand the text?	Do I understand the text?	Do I understand the text?	Do I understand the text?
What pictures do I see in my mind's eye?	What pictures do I see in my mind's eye?	What pictures do I see in my mind's eye?	What pictures do I see in my mind's eye?
What experiences of my own does the text remind me of?	What experiences of my own does the text remind me of?	What experiences of my own does the text remind me of?	What experiences of my own does the text remind me of?
What do I think about the text?	What do I think about the text?	What do I think about the text?	What do I think about the text?
What information that I already know is related to this new information?	What information that I already know is related to this new information?	What information that I already know is related to this new information?	What information that I already know is related to this new information?
What questions do I still have?	What questions do I still have?	What questions do I still have?	What questions do I still have?
Why is this information important?	Why is this information important?	Why is this information important?	Why is this information important?
How could I use this information in the future?	How could I use this information in the future?	How could I use this information in the future?	How could I use this information in the future?
What do I think the next paragraph will discuss?	What do I think the next paragraph will discuss?	What do I think the next paragraph will discuss?	What do I think the next paragraph will discuss?

What to Do When You Don't Understand

Can you tell when you do *not* understand what you are reading? It is a common occurrence, even for the most skilled readers. Here are some clues you can learn to recognize:

1. You are thinking about some activity you plan to do.
2. You are falling asleep.
3. The text refers you to a concept already presented, but you do not remember it.
4. You finish the reading assignment, but you remember nothing of what you just read.

If you have trouble recognizing when you are stuck, get in the habit of stopping reading every few paragraphs. Try to tell yourself what you just read. If you cannot do it, you did not understand what you just read. You are stuck.

Successful readers often get stuck. However, they are different from unsuccessful readers in the following way: Successful readers apply "fix-up strategies" when they get stuck. These fix-up strategies help them figure out the meaning of the text. You can be a successful reader by learning and using fix-up strategies. Here are some suggestions.

Fix-Up Strategies for Reading

1. Go back to the sentence or paragraph where you last understood the text. Go over in your mind what that text means or what you learned from that text. Use your "Questions to Ask While Reading" bookmark to ask yourself questions about the text and answer them.

2. Look at the first paragraph of text that you did not understand. Ask yourself, "Why do I not understand this text?" Try to verbalize the reasons that you do not understand the text. The following are some reasons and fix-up strategies.

3. There are one or more words that you do not know. First, find the word in your textbook's glossary. Read the definition. Use the index to find where the term was first used, and reread that section of text to help you understand the term. If the word is not in your textbook's glossary, use a dictionary to learn the meaning of the word. Copy the word, its definition, and the sample usage into your vocabulary notebook, so that you will remember it next time you see it. You might also enter the word into an Internet search engine, along with the word *definition*. The search engine should provide you with several definitions and sample usages.

4. If the text has a description, try to visualize what is being described. If steps of a process are described, imagine yourself doing the process as you read each step.

5. Do the words in the text remind you of any experiences you have had? Think about those experiences and how they might apply to this section of text.

6. Make a diagram of the information in the text.

7. Reread the text more slowly. Then explain to yourself the meaning of the text, based on the strategies that you used.

8. If you still do not understand the text, find a partner. Read the text together and use the above strategies. If the two of you still do not understand, arrange to meet with the teacher to help you.

Activity Buffet: Role Plays

Role Plays
Teacher's Guidelines

Situation

1. Organize students into groups of three or four, and give each student a copy of the "Role-Play Record Sheet." Have the groups review the chapter in the textbook that you are currently studying. Tell each group to develop a situation for a role play, based on the chapter content. You might want to explain the items requested on the record sheet and model an example for them, for example,

    Setting. The place where the role play takes place, for example, a clothing store.

    Problem or Conflict. The issue or basis for the interaction in the role play, for example, a customer wants to return a shirt for cash.

    Constraints. An external rule or situation that influences or controls how the people in the role play respond, for example, company policy is to accept returns for credit only, not cash.

2. Have groups share their situation ideas and discuss. Have students revise or finalize their responses on the "Situation" section of their record sheets.

Roles

3. Have groups fill out the "Roles" section of their record sheets. Have groups share the roles, and help students refine or clarify the roles.

Observer

4. Explain the role of the observer. Have groups brainstorm the types of behaviors and attitudes that the observer should look for and discuss. Students might list the behaviors and attitudes to look for, such as empathy, respect, humor, positive attitude, promptness, thoroughness, knowledge.

Playing the Role Play

5. Have students do the role plays in their small groups with only one or two observers. By doing so, the amount of "stage fright" is significantly reduced. When every group has completed its role play, ask a group to volunteer to perform theirs for the whole class and use it as the basis of a whole class discussion.

6. A successful role play has three parts: preparation, performance, and analysis. The amount of time necessary for each part varies, depending on the topic and the students. A rough estimate is 20 minutes for the introduction, discussion, and filling out the record sheet. Allow about five minutes for performing the role play and five minutes for the analysis. Have students switch roles and perform the role play again, another 10 minutes. Have a volunteer group perform their role play for the whole class, another five minutes. Then have a whole class discussion, 10 to 20 minutes.

7. Have each student write a reaction paper for the role play. You can use the "Reaction Paper" form in the *Activity Buffet—Communication.*

Activity Buffet: Role Plays

Role-Play Record Sheet

Name____ **Date** _____________ **Period** _______

Situation

- **Setting (where the role play takes place):**____

- **Problem or Conflict (issue or basis for the interaction):** _________________________________

  ____

  ____

- **Constraints (external rules or situations that influence or control how the people in the role play respond):**____

  ____

  ____

Roles

There should be two roles in the role play. Name each role, such as salesperson and angry customer. Describe role (person), such as what his or her job is, personality, and person's goal in the interaction.

Role 1 Name: ____

Role 1 Description: ____

____

____

Role 2 Name: ____

Role 2 Description: ____

____

____

Observer

Describe the behaviors or attitudes that could be improved: ________________________________

____

____

____

____

____

Activity Buffet: Vocabulary

Vocabulary: Individual or Group

Definition Predictions. On a piece of paper, write each word from the Marketing Terms list. Then write what you think the definition of each word is. Compare your definition with the definition in the text. Write the word and its correct definition in your vocabulary notebook.

Dictionary Definitions. For each word in the Marketing Terms list, copy the word into your vocabulary notebook. Then copy the word's definition.

Your Own Definitions. For each word in the Marketing Terms list, write the definition in your own words. Use examples or diagrams to help you.

Sentences. For each word in the Marketing Terms list, find a sentence in the text that contains the word. Copy that sentence into your vocabulary notebook. Then write your own sentence that uses the word.

Word Derivations. Look up each word in the Marketing Terms list in an unabridged dictionary. Write down the derivation of the word. Write a sentence or two that explains how the source of the word is related to its current meaning. Find at least two other words that have similar source words. Explain in writing how the meanings of all three words are related to each other and to the source word or words.

Words in the News. Find an article on a topic covered in the chapter. Look in newspapers, news magazines *(Time, Newsweek, US News and World Report)*, or business magazines *(Business Week, Fortune, Forbes, Nation's Business)*. Read the article. Look for the words in the Marketing Terms list and write them in your vocabulary notebook. Copy each sentence containing the word into your vocabulary notebook. Then rewrite each sentence in your own words.

Flash Cards. You will need a stack of index cards. For each word on the Marketing Terms list, write the word on one side of an index card. Write its definition on the other side. Use the flash cards to test your knowledge. Use the word side to read the word, then tell the definition. Use the definition side to read the definition, then tell and spell the word.

Explanations. Imagine that you are hosting a student from another country. In writing, explain each word in the Marketing Terms list to your guest. Feel free to use examples, drawings, and diagrams to help you.

Word Search. Create a word search on a piece of graph paper. Use the words in the Marketing Terms list. Make a copy without the answers to exchange with a partner.

Crossword Puzzle. Create a crossword puzzle on a piece of graph paper. Use the words in the Marketing Terms list. Be sure to number the words and include a definition for each word. Make a blank copy to exchange with a partner.

Fairy Tale. Choose a nursery rhyme or fairy tale. Rewrite it in today's language and use the words in the chapter's Marketing Terms list. Share your rewritten fairy tale.

Word Pairs. Study the words in the terms list. Organize the words into pairs. (You can also use your flashcards to pair the words.) On a sheet of paper, record your pairs. Then write a sentence or two explaining why you put the words together. Here are some ways that words can be related: same, similar, opposites, both words are part of the same thing, one word is part of the other word, one word is the result of the other word. For example, domestic – foreign are opposites.

Word Categories. Study the words in the terms list. Organize the words into categories. (You can use your flashcards to organize the words.) On a sheet of paper, record your categories. Give each category a name. For each category, explain why the words fit into that category. For example, one category is Product. The words in that category are good, service, and idea. Good, service, and idea are all products. Products are something that a customer can buy.

Vocabulary: Group

Hangman. Organize students into small groups. Choose one person in each group to be the first hangman. The hangman secretly selects a word from the chapter's concept list. On a piece of paper or board that all can see, the hangman makes a dash for each letter in the word he or she chose. One by one, each member of the group guesses which letters are in the word. If a correct letter is guessed, the hangman writes it on the proper dash in the word. If the letter is incorrect, the hangman draws part of a stick figure. (The stick figure has six parts: head, trunk, two arms, two legs.) The group guesses letters until the correct word is identified or until a complete person is drawn. If the group correctly identifies the word, they get a point. If they also correctly define the word, they get a second point. When the word is correctly identified and defined, or a complete person is drawn, the game starts again with a new hangman.

Concentration. This game works best for terms lists with eight or more terms. Organize students into groups. Give each group index cards equal to twice the number of terms. Have the group write each term on one card, then the definition for each term on another card. Have students place all cards face down, mix up the order, then arrange the cards neatly in rows. Have the group select one member as the monitor. Give the monitor the list of words with their correct definitions. Have students determine the order of play (clockwise, birth dates). The first student turns over one card and reads the word or definition. The student then turns over another card. If the word and definition match, then the student takes the two cards. The monitor checks the list to make sure the term and definition are correct. If they do not match, then the play passes to the next person. Play continues until all the cards are picked up. The person with the most cards wins.

What Was the Question? This game is based on the game "Jeopardy." Organize students into groups. Have each group make a terms list with definitions. Organize the groups into pairs. Have one group read definitions to the other group. The other group must give the word in the form of a question, for example, "What is *utility*?"

Tic-Tac-Mark and **Charades.** Both these games work well with vocabulary. See instructions in *Activity Buffet—Games.*

Snowball. Divide a large vocabulary list among your students so that each term is assigned to at least one student, but no more than three students. Give each student one colored slip of paper and one white slip of paper. Have the students write the term on the white paper and its definition on the colored slip of paper. Have students scrunch each paper into a snowball. Designate a clear area of the room that is large enough for students to access easily. Have students throw all their snowballs into this area. Then give students the opportunity to pick up the snowballs and match the term to its correct definition. When all the terms have been matched, have students read their terms and definitions to the class.

Quotations and Sayings

Write one of the following on the board or an overhead. Ask students to explain what the quote or saying means, and say whether they agree with the quote. You could also ask them to describe a situation to which the quote or saying can be applied, and then explain how the quote or saying applies. Note: For additional quotations and sayings, enter "Quotations" and a topic, such as "happiness" or "leadership" or "motivation," into an Internet search engine.

"Not everything that can be counted counts, and not everything that counts can be counted." Albert Einstein

"We are all angels with only one wing; we can only fly while embracing one another." Luciano de Crescenzo

"Yard by yard, it's pretty hard. Inch by inch, it's a cinch." Unknown

"Winning isn't everything, but wanting to win is." Vince Lombardi

"Friendship with oneself is all important because without it one cannot be friends with anybody else in the world." Eleanor Roosevelt

"Learning without thought is labor lost; thought without learning is perilous." Confucius

"Smooth seas do not make skillful sailors." African Proverb

"Troubles, like babies, grow larger by nursing." Lady Holland

"Nothing is particularly hard if you divide it into small jobs." Henry Ford

"Though no one can go back and make a brand new start, anyone can start from now and make a brand new end." Unknown

"Chance favors the prepared mind." Louis Pasteur

"A camel is a horse designed by committee." Unknown

"To fly, we have to have resistance." Maya Lin

"Remember that time is money." Benjamin Franklin

"An optimist sees an opportunity in every calamity. A pessimist sees a calamity in every opportunity." Unknown

"When one door shuts, another opens." Spanish Proverb

"The expert in anything was once a beginner." Unknown

"It's your attitude, not your aptitude, that determines your altitude." Unknown

"In the long run, the pessimist may be proved right, but the optimist has a better time on the trip." Daniel Reardon

"If you keep saying things are going to be bad, you have a good chance of being a prophet." Isaac Singer

"Snowflakes are frail, but if enough of them get together, they can stop traffic." Vance Havner

"The thing about our choices is that after we have made them, they turn around and make us." Unknown

"Be the change you wish to see in the world." Ghandi

Warm-Up Ideas

Ad. Bring in a print ad, and post it at the front of the room or display it on an overhead. Have students describe in writing their reactions to the ad. How would they improve it?

Words to Know. Find a list of words high school students should know. Assign one word to a student for each day. That student is responsible for sharing the definition and an example of the word used in a sentence. Each student must copy the definition and example sentence in a vocabulary notebook, then write his or her own sentence using the word.

Marketing I've Seen Today. Have students describe in writing all the examples of marketing that they have seen so far today.

Reality Checks. Have students work in groups to answer all the Reality Checks in a chapter.

Photo Analysis. Assign one of the photos from the current chapter. Have students write a description of the photo, then explain why the photo is used in the book at this point.

Chapter Reflection. Have students write their answers to "Why do you think the information in this chapter is important? How might you use the information in this chapter in the future?"

Grateful Cards. Give students colored 4 x 6 index cards or create your own from colored construction paper cut into quarters. Have students write in large letters at the top "I am grateful for . . . . " then tell students to complete the sentence by writing one thing in their lives that they are truly grateful for. If students are stumped the first time you do this, have a general class discussion. Help students realize that they might be grateful for things that they take for granted, such as the ability to see or their parents or friends.

Fifty Years Ago. Use the Internet to find the cost of a common item 50 years ago, such as a McDonald's hamburger. Find the price today. Have students calculate the percentage increase.

Math for the Day. Consult the almanac section of the newspaper or the "X Years Ago" section of a magazine, such as *Scientific American*. Tell the students to listen very carefully while you read the story or information to them. Ahead of time, embed some information that you will ask students to remember and use in a simple math problem. For example, you might read them the story of the sinking of the Titanic. At the end, ask them how many people died and how many survived. Ask them how long ago the catastrophe took place. The first time, many students may not be able to do it, because they were not listening carefully. However, the more often you do this activity, the better your students will get at noticing the important information and remembering it.

What Happened Yesterday? Ask a student to describe what the class did yesterday, while you take attendance or attend to other administrative tasks. The first time you do this, students may have a hard time remembering. However, the more often you do it, the better students will get at it. This activity also is helpful for anyone who was absent.

Make a Mark. Ask a volunteer to come to the board and draw (make a mark) on the board something that illustrates what the class did yesterday. Have class members guess what the drawing means.

What's New? Ask, "Did you see anything new today (or last week)?" Help student focus on new products or advertising, such as a new sandwich at a fast-food restaurant, a new commercial for an established product, or new car models.

Activity Buffet: Workplace/Job Search Skills

What Do Employers Expect of Me as an Employee?

- Come to work every day on time.
- Follow directions.
- Apply good listening skills.
- Concentrate on my work.
- Recognize problems and find solutions.
- Manage time effectively.
- Maintain a safe work environment.
- Be honest and dependable.
- Dress properly and practice good grooming.
- Be cooperative.
- Have a positive attitude.

Source: Poster, *What Do Employers Expect of Me as an Employee?* CWI Workforce Investment Board Youth Council, developed as result of a Department of Workforce Development Grant.

Activity Buffet: Workplace/Job Search Skills

Explore Want Ads

Obtain the "Help Wanted" section of your local paper. The Sunday editions usually have the largest number of ads. Find a want ad for a marketing job that appeals to you. Here are some of the headings under which you will find marketing jobs: Advertising, Buyer, Customer Service, Manager, Market Research, Marketing Communications, Purchasing, Retail Sales, Sales, Shipping/Receiving, Telemarketing, Warehouse. Read the ad, then answer these questions. After you answer the questions, tape the ad to your paper.

1. **Why did the ad appeal to you?**

2. **What is the job title?**

3. **What is the name of the company?**

4. **What does the company do?**

5. **Where is the company located?**

6. **What does the ad tell you about the work environment?**

7. **Does the company sound like a place you would enjoy working? Why or why not?**

8. **What are the requirements for the job?**

9. **Are you currently qualified for the job? If not, what would you have to do to qualify for the job? (Describe schooling and jobs you would need to have already had.)**

10. **What are the job tasks?**

11. **Which functions of marketing would you perform?**

12. **What impact would you have on the business?**

13. **What personal qualities should a person in this job have?**

14. **What is the salary?**

15. **How should you contact the company?**

16. **If you were interested in the job, what would you do?**

17. **Are you interested in this job? Why or why not?**

Activity Buffet: Workplace/Job Search Skills

What Are Your Workplace Skills?

Name_______________________________________ **Date** _____________ **Period** _______

Workplace Skills	Very Good	Good	Fair	Poor	Do Not Possess
Basic Skills					
Read written material, charts, and graphs.					
Write an effective letter.					
Calculate a percentage discount on a product.					
Speak to a group.					
Listen to instructions to complete a new task.					
Thinking Skills					
Learn new job responsibilities.					
Use reasoning skills to choose from alternatives.					
Use creative thinking to develop a new idea.					
Make decisions about work priorities.					
Apply established procedures to new projects.					
Resource Skills					
Manage time well.					
Organize work and storage spaces.					
Use a budget for money management.					
Use supplies and tools wisely.					
Divide work according to group members' skills.					
Interpersonal Skills					
Contribute to group efforts.					
Teach others new skills.					
Lead others in a project.					
Negotiate with others to gain an agreement.					
Work well with others from different cultures.					
Information Skills					
Research and collect data from reliable sources.					
Organize and maintain a file system.					
Give a speech using various media.					
Interpret instructions on a work procedure.					
Use a computer to create documents.					
System Skills					
Explain and draw an organizational chart.					
Diagram the steps of a problem's possible solutions.					
Propose a plan for a situation needing change.					
Monitor, correct, and improve your work performance.					
Break down a complex task into component parts.					
Technology Skills					
Judge the best procedures, tools, or machines to use.					
Assemble equipment from instructions.					
Operate equipment according to guidelines.					
Identify reasons for wrong results from tools or machines.					
Follow maintenance procedures to prevent failures.					

(Continues)

Name____ **Date** _____________ **Period** _______

Circle your five strongest skills from the choices given. How did you acquire these skills?

____

____

____

____

____

____

How can you improve the *Fair* or *Poor* skills you identified?

____

____

____

____

____

____

____

How can you acquire the skills you do not possess?

____

____

____

____

____

How will your skills influence your career choice?

____

____

____

____

____

____

Resources

Bibliography

Assessment

Burke, Kay. *The Mindful School: How to Assess Authentic Learning.* 5th ed. Thousand Oaks, CA: Corwin Press, 2009.

Herman, Joan L.; Aschbacher, Pamela R.; Winters, Lynn. *A Practical Guide to Alternative Assessment.* Alexandria, VA: Association for Supervision and Curriculum Development, 1992.

Rucker, Jim, ed. *Assessment in Business Education.* Reston, VA: National Business Education Association, 2000.

Stevens, Danielle D.; Levi, Antonia. *Introduction to Rubrics.* Sterling, VA: Stylus Publishing, LLC, 2005.

Classroom Management

Marshall, Marvin. *Discipline Without Stress.* 2nd ed. See www.disciplinewithoutstress.com.

Powell, Angela. *The Cornerstone: Classroom Management That Makes Teaching More Effective, Efficient, and Enjoyable.* Florida: Due Season Press, 2009. See www.thecornerstoneforteachers.com.

Wong, Harry and Rosemary. *Effective Teaching.* Series of articles on the Web site Teachers.net. Click on link, "Harry Wong."

Wong, Harry and Rosemary. *The First Days of School.* 4th ed. See www.effectiveteaching.com.

Cooperative Learning

Benson, Barbara P. *How to Meet Standards, Motivate Students, and (Still) Enjoy Teaching!: Four Practices That Improve Student Learning.* 2nd ed. Thousand Oaks, CA: Corwin Press, 2008.

Johnson, David R.; Johnson, Roger T. *Learning Together and Alone: Cooperative, Competitive, and Individualistic Learning.* 5th ed. Merrill Publishing, 1999.

Kagan, Spencer. *Cooperative Learning.* See www.kaganonline.com

Rogers, Spence; Ludington, Jim; Graham, Shari. *Motivation and Learning.* Peak Learning Systems, Inc., 1999. See www.peaklearn.com

Electronic Newsletters

NSGA Research News: Free E-Mail Newsletter. Mount Prospect, IL: National Sporting Goods Association. http://nsga.org/public/pages/index.cfm?pageid=340.

SmartBrief: Free E-Mail Newsletter. Washington, DC: National Retail Federation. http://www.smartbrief.com/nrf/.

STORES Magazine: Monthly Publication. Washington, DC: National Retail Federation. http://www.stores.org/.

VisualStore Dispatch: Free E-Mail Newsletter. Cincinnati, OH: ST Media Group International. http://www.visualstore.com/join.php.

Ethics

Blanchard, Kenneth H.; Peale, Norman Vincent. *The Power of Ethical Management.* HarperCollins Publishers, 1988.

DesJardins, Joseph R. *An Introduction to Business Ethics.* 3rd ed. The McGraw-Hill Companies, 2009.

Maxwell, John C. *Leadership 101: What Every Leader Needs to Know.* Nashville, TN: Center Street, 2005.

Positive Attitude

Canfield, Jack (editor); Kirberger, Kimberly; Hansen, Mark Victor. *Chicken Soup for the Teenage Soul (series)*. Deerfield, FL: Health Communications, Incorporated, 1997–2008.

Disney Institute; Eisner, Michael D. *Be Our Guest: Perfecting the Art of Customer Service*. Disney Press, 2003.

Fish video, www.fishphilosophy.com

Lundin, Stephen C.; Paul, Harry; Christensen, John. *Fish! A Remarkable Way to Boost Morale and Improve Results*. New York: Hyperion, 2000.

Seuss, Dr. *Oh, The Places You'll Go!* New York: Random House, Inc., 1990.

Spector, Robert; McCarthy, Patrick. *The Nordstrom Way to Customer Service Excellence*. John Wiley & Sons, 2005.

Reading, Writing, Study Skills

Allen, Janet. *Tools for Teaching Content Literacy*. Portland, MN: Stenhouse Publishers, 2004.

Blachowicz, Camille; Ogle, Donna. *Reading Comprehension: Strategies for Independent Learners*. New York: Guilford Press, 2001.

Daniels, Harvey; Zemelman, Steven. *Subjects Matter: Every Teacher's Guide to Content-Area Reading*. Portsmouth, NH: Heinemann, 2004.

Goldberg, Donna. *The Organized Student: Teaching Children the Skills for Success in School and Beyond*. New York: Fireside, 2005.

Glenn, Joanne Lozar, ed. "Strengthening Basic Skills." *Keying In: The Newsletter of the National Business Education Association* 16, no. 2, (November 2005).

Tovani, Chris. *I Read It, but I Don't Get It*. Portland, MN: Stenhouse Publishers, 2000.

Tovani, Chris. *Do I Really Have to Teach Reading? Content Comprehension, Grades 6–12*. Portland, MN: Stenhouse Publishers, 2004.

www.englishcompanion.com. Although this Web site is aimed at English teachers, there are many excellent tools and ideas for teachers in all subjects. Search the site for topics such as "note-taking."

Robert's Rules of Order

Roberts, Ru; Robert III, Henry M.; Evans, William J.; Honemann, Daniel H. *Robert's Rules of Order*. 10th ed. New York: HarperCollins, 2000.

SparkNotes. *Robert's Rules of Order*. New York: Spark Publishing, 2006.

Zimmerman, Doris P. *Robert's Rules in Plain English*. 2nd ed. New York: HarperCollins, 2005.

Teaching Strategies

Glenn, Joanne Lozar, ed. "Project Based Learning." *Keying In: Newsletter of the National Business Education Association* 16, no. 3 (January 2006).

Scherer, Marge, ed. "The Constructivist Classroom." *Journal of the Association for Supervision and Curriculum Development* 57, no. 3 (November 1999).

Teachers.net. This Web site is billed as "the ultimate teacher resource."

Technology

Glenn, Joanne Lozar. "Blogging for Teaching and Learning." In *Business Education Forum* 59, no. 2, (December 2004), pages 9–13.

www.netsmartz.org This Web site is an interactive, educational safety resource from the National Center for Missing & Exploited Children and Boys & Girls Clubs of America for children aged 5 to 17, parents, guardians, educators, and law enforcement. It uses age-appropriate 3-D activities to teach children how to stay safer on the Internet.

Additional Resources

The following lists include sources of information and materials that may be useful to you and your students. Please note that information provided here was correct at time of publication. It may have changed since then.

Note: Phone numbers and Web addresses may have changed since publication. For some entries, reaching the correct Web site may require keying **www.** in front of the listed Web address.

Publications

Current magazines and journals are good sources of information and examples of marketing. The education journals can provide tips for presenting concepts and managing the classroom. Students will find many of these publications useful for activities suggested in the *Marketing Dynamics* program. Many of these publications are available in the periodicals section of your public library.

Business/Marketing/Entrepreneurship

Advertising Age
adage.com

American Demographics
adage.com/americandemographics

Black Enterprise
blackenterprise.com

Billboard
billboard.com
billboard.biz

Business Ethics
business-ethics.com

BusinessWeek
businessweek.com

The Economist
economist.com

Entrepreneur
entrepreneur.com

Fast Company
fastcompany.com

Forbes
forbes.com

Fortune
fortune.com

Hispanic Business
hispanicbusiness.com

Home Business
homebusinessmag.com

Inc.
inc.com

Money
money.com

Sales & Marketing Management
salesandmarketing.com

SmartMoney: The Wall Street Journal Magazine
smartmoney.com

Wall Street Journal
wsj.com

Education

The Black Child Advocate
(202) 833-2220
nbcdi.org

Business Education Forum
(703) 860-8300
nbea.org

Educational Leadership
(800) 933-ASCD
ascd.org

The Education Digest
eddigest.com

Education Resources Information Center (ERIC)
(800) 538-3742
ed.gov

Exceptional Children
(888) CEC-SPED
cec.sped.org

Instructor
(212) 343-6100
scholastic.com/instructor

Keying In: The Newsletter of the National Business Education Association
(703) 860-8300
nbea.org

General/Consumer

AARP: The Magazine
aarpmagazine.org

Better Homes and Gardens
bhg.com

Congressional Digest
congressionaldigestcorp.com

Consumer Reports
consumerreports.org

Consumer Action Handbook
(888) 878-3256
consumeraction.gov

Discover: Science, Technology and The Future
discovermagazine.com

Ebony Magazine
ebonyjet.com

Essence Magazine
essence.com

The Family Handyman
familyhandyman.com

FDA Consumer: The Magazine of the U.S. Food and Drug Administration
fda.gov/FDAC

Foreign Affairs
foreignaffairs.org

The Futurist
wfs.org

Hispanic Magazine
hispaniconline.com

Home Magazine
homemag.com

Latina Style Magazine
latinastyle.com

National Geographic Traveler
nationalgeographic.com/traveler

Newsweek
newsweek.com

The New York Times
nytimes.com

PC Magazine
pcmag.com

Popular Mechanics
popularmechanics.com

Popular Science
popsci.com

Science News
sciencenews.org

Scientific American
sciam.com

Technology Review
technologyreview.com

Time
time.com

TrailerLife
trailerlife.com

Training
trainingmag.com

USA Today
usatoday.com

U.S. News & World Report
usnews.com

Working Mother
workingmother.com

Business, Consumer, and Educational Organizations

Trade and professional organizations often provide helpful information on issues of industry-wide importance. Marketing is important to most of these organizations, for recruiting members, educating the public, and influencing legislators and voters. Many of these organizations publish print journals or newsletters and have Web sites.

Business/ Entrepreneurship/Marketing

American Apparel and Footwear Association
(800) 520-2262
apparelandfootwear.org

American Arbitration Association
(212) 484-4000
adr.org

American Bankers Association
(800) 226-5377
aba.com

American Bar Association
(312) 988-5522
abanet.org

American Concrete Institute
(248) 848-3700
aci-int.org

American Council of Life Insurers
(202) 624-2000
acli.com

American Design Drafting Association
(731) 627-0802
adda.org

American Financial Services Association
(202) 296-5544
afsaonline.org

American Fiber Manufacturers Association, Inc.
(703) 875-0432
fibersource.com

American Gas Association
(202) 824-7000
aga.org

American Hardware Manufacturers Association
(847) 605-1025
ahma.org

American Lighting Association
(800) 605-4448
americanlightingassoc.com

American Marketing Association
(800) AMA-1150
marketingpower.com

American Medical Association
(312) 464-5000
ama-assn.org

American Plastics Council
(703) 741-5000
plasticsinfo.org

American Plywood Association
(253) 565-6600
apawood.org

American Society for Testing and Materials (ASTM)
(610) 832-9585
astm.org

American Society of Furniture Designers
(910) 576-1273
asfd.com

American Society of Interior Designers
(202) 546-3480
asid.org

American Textile Manufacturers Institute, Inc.
(202) 862-0500
atmi.org

American Wool Council—American Sheep Industry Association
(303) 771-3500
sheepusa.org

Architectural Woodwork Institute
(703) 733-0600
awinet.org

Association of Home Appliance Manufacturers
(202) 872-5955
aham.org

California Redwood Association
(888) 225-7339
calredwood.org

Chamber of Commerce of the United States of America
(202) 659-6000
uschamber.com

Cotton Inc.
(212) 413-8300
cottoninc.com

Council of Better Business Bureaus, Inc.
(703) 276-0100
bbb.org

Crafted with Pride in the USA Council, Inc.
craftedwithpride.org

Credit Union National Association, Inc.
(800) 356-9655
cuna.org

Edward Lowe Foundation (entrepreneurship)
edwardlowe.org

Food Marketing Institute
(202) 452-8444
fmi.org

The Foundation for Entrepreneurship (Ewing Marion Kauffman Foundation)
kauffman.org

Grocery Manufacturers Association
(202) 337-9400
gmabrands.com

HomeBusinessOnline
homebusinessonline.com

International Association of Lighting Designers
(312) 527-3677
iald.org

National Association of Home Builders
(800) 368-5242
nahb.com

National Association of the Remodeling Industry
(800) 611-6274
nari.org

Kitchen Cabinet Manufacturers Association
(703) 264-1690
kcma.org

Manufactured Housing Institute
(703) 558-0400
manufacturedhousing.org

National Cotton Council of America
(901) 274-9030
cotton.org

National Council of Better Business Bureaus
(703) 276-0100
bbb.org

National Dairy Council
(800) 426-8271
nationaldairycouncil.org

National Restaurant Association
(202) 331-5900
restaurant.org

National Safety Council
(630) 285-1121
nsc.org

Soap and Detergent Association
(202) 347-2900
cleaning101.com

Sustainable Buildings Industries Council
(202) 628-7400
sbicouncil.org

Underwriters Laboratories, Inc.
(847) 272-8800
ul.com

United States Association for Small Business and Entrepreneurship
(561) 297-4060
usasbe.org

Women Entrepreneurs, Inc
we-inc.org

Women's Business Center
womensbiz.org

Wool Bureau, Inc.
(212) 221-8161
wool.com

Consumer

American Cancer Society
(800) ACS-2345
cancer.org

American Council on Consumer Interests
(414) 918-3189
consumerinterests.org

American Council on Exercise (ACE)
(800) 825-3636
acefitness.org

American Diabetes Association
(800) 342-2383
diabetes.org

American Dietetic Association (ADA)
(800) 877-1600
eatright.org

American Lung Association
(800) LUNG-USA
lungusa.org

American Red Cross
(202) 303-5000
redcross.org

American Savings Education Council
(202) 659-0670
choosetosave.org/asec/

Boys and Girls Clubs of America
(404) 487-5700
bgca.org

Center for Science in the Public Interest (CSPI)
(202) 332-9110
cspinet.org

Consumer Federation of America
(202) 387-6121
consumerfed.org

Consumers Union
(914) 378-2000
consumersunion.org

Insurance Information Institute
(212) 346-5500
iii.org

Internet Fraud Watch
fraud.org

Jump$tart Coalition for Personal Financial Literacy
(888) 45-EDUCATE
jumpstart.org

National Consumer Law Center
(617) 542-8010
consumerlaw.org

National Consumers League
(202) 835-3323
natlconsumersleague.org

National Foundation for Credit Counseling
(301) 589-5600
nfcc.org

National Fraud Information Center
fraud.org

National Insurance Consumer Helpline
iii.org

National Taxpayers Union
(703) 683-5700
ntu.org

Shape Up America!
shapeup.org

Education

American Educational Research Association (AERA)
(202) 238-3200
aera.net

Association for Career and Technical Education (ACTE)
(800) 826-9972
acteonline.org

Association for Supervision and Curriculum Development (ASCD)
(800) 933-ASCD
ascd.org

Council for Exceptional Children
(888) CEC-SPED
cec.sped.org

Consortium for Entrepreneurship Education
(614) 486-6538
entre-ed.org

Creative Education Foundation
(800) 447-2774
creativeeducationfoundation.org

MBA Research & Curriculum Center
(800) 448-0398
mbaresearch.org/

International Reading Association
(800) 336-READ
reading.org

International Technology Education Association
(703) 860-2100
iteaconnect.org

National Association for Gifted Children
(202) 785-4268
nagc.org

National Business Education Association
(703) 860-8300
nbea.org

National Council on Economic Education
(800) 338-1192
ncee.net

National Education Association (NEA)
(202) 833-4000
nea.org

National Foundation for Teaching Entrepreneurship (NFTE)
(800) FOR-NFTE
nfte.org

National Information Center for Children and Youth with Disabilities
(800) 695-0285
nichcy.org

National Marketing Education Association
(602) 750-6735
nationalmea.org

Society for Research in Child Development
srcd.org

Students Against Destructive Decisions (SADD)
(877) SADD-INC
saddonline.org/

Company Resources

Companies often provide materials that showcase their products and compare them with similar products in the marketplace. Some companies also provide generic educational materials on topics related to their products. All of these companies have Web sites worth analyzing for their consumer or B2B appeal.

Alcoa Building Products
(800) 962-6973
alcoahomes.com

Amana Refrigeration
(866) 616-2664
amana.com

American Olean Tile Co.
americanolean.com

American Stock Exchange, Inc.
(212) 306-1000
amex.com

Andersen Windows
(651) 264-5150
andersenwindows.com

AristOKraft
(717) 359-4131
aristokraft.com

Armstrong World Industries Inc.
(800) 233-3823
armstrongfloors.com

BASF Corp.
(973) 245-6013
basf.com

Benjamin Moore
(800) 344-0400
benjaminmoore.com

Bernina of America Inc.
berninausa.com

Black and Decker
(800) 762-6672
blackanddecker.com

Brown Jordan International
(800) 743-4252
brownjordan.com

Bruce Hardwood Floors
(800) 233-3823
bruce.com

Burlington Industries Inc.
(336) 379-4675
burlington.com

Butterick Company, Inc.
(800) 782-0323
butterick.com

Carrier Air Conditioning Co.
(800) 227-7437
carrier.com

Clorox Co.
(800) 292-2200
clorox.com

Colgate-Palmolive Co.
(800) 468-6502
colgate.com

Congoleum Corp.
(800) 274-3266
congoleum.com

Cuisinart
(800) 211-9604
cuisinart.com

Delta Faucets Co.
(800) 345-3358
deltafaucet.com

Dow Chemical USA
(800) 258-2436
dow.com

Dow Jones Indexes
(212) 597-5720
djindexes.com

Dupont Fibers
(800) 441-7515
dupont.com

Ethan Allen Inc.
(888) EAHELP1
ethanallen.com

Faultless Starch/Bon Ami Co.
bonami.com

Frigidaire
(800) 374-4432
frigidaire.com

F. Schumacher & Co.
(800) 523-1200
fschumacher.com

GE Appliances
(800) 626-2005
geappliances.com

Georgia-Pacific Corp.
(800) 284-5347
gp.com

Haan Crafts Corporation
(800) 422-6548
haancrafts.com

Hoover Co.
(800) 944-9200
hoover.com

Hunter Douglas
(800) 366-4327
hunterdouglas.com

Jenn-Air
(800) JENN-AIR
jennair.com

Kirsch
(866) 469-9200
kirsch.com

KitchenAid
(800) 541-6390
kitchenaid.com

Kohler Co.
(800) 456-4537
kohler.com

KraftMaid Cabinetry
(888) 562-7744
kraftmaid.com

Lane Furniture
lanefurniture.com

Laufen
(800) 321-0684
laufenusa.com

Lennox Industries Inc.
(800) 9-LENNOX
davelennox.com

Levolor Home Fashion
(800) 538-6567
levolor.com

Magic Chef-Maytag Appliance Co.
(800) 688-1120
maytag.com

Mannington Mills, Inc.
(800) 356-6787
mannington.com

Marvin Windows
(800) 328-0268
marvin.com

Masco Corp.
(313) 274-7400
masco.com

Maytag Appliance Co.
(800) 688-9900
maytag.com

McCall Pattern Company
(800) 782-0323
mccall.com

Mills Pride
(800) 441-0337
reps.millspride.com

Minwax/Sherwin-Williams
(800) 523-9299
minwax.com

NASDAQ
nasdaq.com

New York Stock Exchange
(212) 656-3000
nyse.com

Nu Tone Inc.
(888) 336-3948
nutone.com

Owens-Corning Fiberglas Corp.
(800) 438-7465
owenscorning.com

Peachtree Doors
(888) 888-3814
peachtreedoor.com

Peerless
(800) 438-6673
peerless-faucet.com

Pella Windows and Doors
(800) 374-4758
pella.com

Pendleton Woolen Mills
(877) 996-6599
pendleton-usa.com

Pfaff American Sales Corp.
(440) 808-6550
pfaffusa.com

Philips Lighting Co.
(800) 555-0050
nam.lighting.philips.com

Jeld-Wen Windows and Doors
(800) 547-6880
jeld-wen.com

Proctor & Gamble Co.
(513) 983-1100
pg.com

Prudential Property & Casualty Co.
(888) 263-6800
prudential.com

Rubbermaid
(888) 895-2110
rubbermaid.com

Sherwin-Williams Co.
(800) 474-3794
sherwin-williams.com

Simplicity Pattern Company, Inc.
(888) 588-2700
simplicity.com

Singer Sewing Co.
(800) 474-6437
singerco.com

Stanley Hardware (Division of the Stanley Works)
(800) 622-4393
stanleyhardware.com

Sunbeam/Oster Household Products
(800) 458-8407
sunbeam.com

Velux-America Inc.
(800)-88-VELUX
veluxusa.com

Viking Sewing Machines
(800) 358-0001
husqvarnaviking.com

Whirlpool Corp.
(800) 253-1301
whirlpool.com

Wood-Mode Inc.
(877) 635-7500
wood-mode.com

Educational Resources

The following companies and associations provide teaching materials as one of their primary missions. Most offer videos and/or computer software, while many offer printed materials. Some have interactive educational Web sites. Contact these organizations for their latest catalogs and prices.

ACT MEDIA
(800) 745-5480
actmedia.org

Agency for Instructional Technology (AIT)
(800) 457-4509
ait.net

American Association for Vocational Instructional Materials (AAVIM)
(800) 228-4689
aavim.org

Bergwall Productions, Inc.
(800) 934-8696
bergwall.com

Cambridge Educational
(800) 257-5126
cambridgeeducational.com

Concept Media
(800) 233-7078
conceptmedia.com

CEV Multimedia
(800) 922-9965
cevmultimedia.com

Durrin Productions
(800) 536-6843
durrinproductions.com

ETR Associates
(831) 438-4060
etr.org

Fasttrac (Business Development Program)
fasttrac.org

Films for the Humanities and Sciences
(800) 257-5126
films.com

Human Relations Media Video (HRM)
(800) 431-2050
hrmvideo.com

Learning Seed
(800) 634-4941
learningseed.com

MBAResearch & Curriculum Center
(800) 448-0398 ext. 0
mbaresearch.org

Media International
(800) 477-7575
mediainternational.com

Meridian Education Corp.
(800) 257-5126
meridian.films.com

Nasco
(800) 558-9595
enasco.com

National Business Education Association (NBEA)
(703) 860-8300
nbea.org

NetSmartz Workshop
netsmartz.org

NIMCO, Inc.
(800) 962-6662
nimcoinc.com

Teenager's Guide to the Real World: Money Really Matters
bygpub.com

Teen Consumer Scrapbook
atg.wa.gov/teenconsumer

YoungBiz
youngbiz.com

Career-Related Organizations and Sites

The following sites provide a wide range of career-related information, including career exploration and planning tools, resume-writing tips, job listings, workplace statistics, and career education information.

America's Career InfoNet
acinet.org

America's Service Locator
servicelocator.org

Association for Career and Technical Education (ACTE)
(800) 826-9972
acteonline.org

Business Professionals of America (BPA)
(614) 895-7277
bpa.org

Career Builder
careerbuilder.com

Career Magazine
careermag.com

CareerOneStop
CareerOneStop.org

Career Resource Center
careers.org

DECA—An Association of Marketing Students
(703) 860-5000
deca.org

Family, Career and Community Leaders of America (FCCLA)
(703) 476-4900
fccla.com

Future Business Leaders of America (FBLA)–Phi Beta Lambda
(800) 325-2946
fbla-pbl.org

Health Occupations Students of America (HOSA)
(800) 321-4672
hosa.org

JobWeb
(800) 544-5272
jobweb.com

Junior Achievement
(800) 843-6395
ja.org

Mapping Your Future
mappingyourfuture.org

Monster
(800) 666-7837
monster.com

MonsterTrak
monstertrak.com

My Future
myfuture.com

National Association of Colleges and Employers JobWeb
jobweb.com

National Dissemination Center for Career and Technical Education
(877) 372-2283
nccte.org

National FFA Organization
(888) 332-2668
ffa.org

Occupational Outlook Handbook
stats.bls.gov/oco

Occupational Outlook Quarterly
(magazine and Web site)
bls.gov/opub/ooq/ooqhome.htm

Occupational Safety and Health Administration (OSHA)
(202) 693-1999
osha.gov

*O*NET Online*
online.onetcenter.org

SkillsUSA
(703) 777-8810
skillsusa.org

Technology Student Association (TSA)
(703) 860-9000
tsawww.org

True Careers
truecareers.com

U.S. Army: Partnership for Youth Success
goarmy.com

U.S. Bureau of Apprenticeship and Training
(877) US-2JOBS
doleta.gov/oa/bat.cfm.cfm

U.S. Bureau of Labor Statistics
(202) 691-5200
stats.bls.gov

U.S. Department of Labor Employment and Training Administration
(877) US-2JOBS
doleta.gov

U.S. Department of Labor Secretary's Commission on Achieving Necessary Skills (SCANS)
wdr.doleta.gov/SCANS

*U.S. Equal Employment Opportunity
  Commission*
  (202) 663-4900
  eeoc.gov

Government Agencies

Government agencies and programs provide information in a wide variety of areas. In addition to information on the Web sites, printed information can be downloaded from the Web site, or you can call the agency and request that printed information be sent to you. Most materials from the federal government are free. The government also uses marketing to promote their programs and educate citizens.

*Board of Governors of the Federal Reserve
  System*
  federalreserve.gov

Bureau of the Census
  (301) 763-INFO
  census.gov

Bureau of the Public Debt
  (800) 722-2678
  publicdebt.treas.gov

CDC National Center for Health Statistics
  (800) 232-4636
  cdc.gov/nchs

*CDC National Center for Injury Prevention
  & Control*
  (800) 232-4636
  cdc.gov/ncipc

*CDC National Prevention Information
  Network*
  (800) 458-5231
  cdcnpin.org

*Centers for Disease Control and Prevention
  (CDC)*
  (800) 232-4636
  cdc.gov

*Consumer Product Safety Commission
  (CPSC)*
  (800) 638-2772
  cpsc.gov

Department of Agriculture (USDA)
  (202) 720-2791
  usda.gov

Department of Commerce (DOC)
  (202) 482-2000
  commerce.gov

Department of Education (ED)
  (800) USA-LEARN
  ed.gov

Department of Energy (DOE)
  (800) 342-5363
  energy.gov

*Department of Health and Human Services
  (HHS)*
  (877) 696-6775
  hhs.gov

*Department of Housing and Urban
  Development (HUD)*
  (202) 708-1112
  hud.gov

Department of the Interior (DOI)
  (202) 208-3100
  doi.gov

Department of Labor (DOL)
  (866) 4USA-DOL
  dol.gov

Department of the Treasury
  (202) 622-2000
  treas.gov

Department of Transportation (DOT)
  (202) 366-4000
  dot.gov

DOE Office of Consumer and Public Liaison
  (800) 342-5363
  eren.doe.gov

Economic Development Administration
  eda.gov

Environmental Protection Agency (EPA)
  (202) 272-0167
  epa.gov

*FDA Center for Food Safety and Applied
  Nutrition Information*
  (888) SAFEFOOD
  foodsafety.gov/list.html

Federal Citizen Information Center (FCIC)
  (888) 878-3256
  pueblo.gsa.gov

Federal Communications Commission (FCC)
  (888) 225-5322
  fcc.gov

*Federal Deposit Insurance Corporation
  (FDIC)*
  (877) 275-3342
  fdic.gov

Federal Trade Commission (FTC)
(877) 382-4357
ftc.gov

Food and Drug Administration (FDA)
(888) 463-6332
fda.gov

FTC Bureau of Consumer Protection
(877) FTC-HELP
ftc.gov/bcp/consumer.shtm

Government Printing Office (GPO)
(866) 512-1800
gpo.gov

Healthfinder–Your Source for Reliable Health Information
healthfinder.gov

HHS Assistant Secretary for Planning and Evaluation
(877) 696-6775
aspe.hhs.gov

Internal Revenue Service (IRS)
(800) 829-1040
irs.ustreas.gov

MyPyramid
(703) 305-7600
mypyramid.gov

National Academy of Sciences
(202) 334-2000
nasonline.org

National Audiovisual Center
(800) 553-6847
ntis.gov

National Cancer Institute
(800) 4-CANCER
nci.nih.gov

National Center for Educational Statistics
(202) 502-7300
nces.ed.gov

National Child Care Information Center
(800) 616-2242
nccic.acf.hhs.gov

National Clearinghouse for Alcohol and Drug Information
(800) 729-6686
ncadi.samhsa.gov

National Council on Disability
(202) 272-2004
ncd.gov

National Health Information Center
(800) 336-4797
health.gov/nhic

National Institute on Aging
(301) 496-1752
nia.nih.gov

National Institutes of Health
(301) 496-4000
nih.gov

National Institute of Mental Health
(301) 443-4513
nimh.nih.gov

Office of Energy Efficiency and Renewable Energy
(800) 363-3732
eren.doe.gov

Office of Fair Housing and Equal Opportunity
(202) 708-1112
hud.gov/offices/fheo

Office of Safe and Drug-Free Schools
(202) 260-3954
ed.gov/about/offices/list/osdfs/index.html

Peace Corps
(800) 424-8580
peacecorps.gov

Postal Service (USPS)
(202) 268-2284
usps.com

President's Council on Physical Fitness and Sports
(202) 690-9000
fitness.gov

Securities and Exchange Commission (SEC)
(888) SEC-6585
sec.gov

Small Business Administration (SBA)
(800) 827-5722
sba.gov

Social Security Administration
(800) 772-1213
ssa.gov

U.S. House of Representatives
house.gov

U.S. Senate
senate.gov

USDA Agricultural Research Service
(301) 504-1074
ars.usda.gov

USDA Center for Nutrition Policy and Promotion
(703) 305-7600
cnpp.usda.gov

USDA Economic Research Service
(202) 694-5050
ers.usda.gov

USDA Food and Nutrition Information Center of the National Agricultural Library
nal.usda.gov/fnic

USDA Food and Nutrition Services
(703) 305-2281
fns.usda.gov/fns

USDA Food Safety and Inspection Service
(800) 535-4555
fsis.usda.gov

USDA School Meals Initiative for Healthy Children
(703) 305-1624
schoolmeals.nal.usda.gov

USDA World Agricultural Outlook Board
(202) 720-5447
usda.gov/oce/commodity/index.htm

Weight-Control Information Network (WIN)
(877) 496-4627
win.niddk.nih.gov

Women-21 (for women entrepreneurs)
women-21.gov